52 Illinois Weekends

GREAT GETAWAYS AND ADVENTURES FOR EVERY SEASON

2nd EDITION

BOB PUHALA

COUNTRY ROADS PRESS
NTC/Contemporary Publishing Group

Library of Congress Cataloging-in-Publication Data

Puhala, Bob.
    52 Illinois weekends : great getaways and adventures for every season
/ Bob Puhala.—2nd ed.
        p.   cm.—(52 weekends)
    Includes index.
    ISBN 1-56626-133-3
    1. Illinois—Guidebooks. I. Title. II. Series.
F539.3.P84   1998
917.7304'43—dc21   98-34155
                                          CIP

Cover and interior design by Nick Panos
Cover and interior illustrations copyright © Jill Banashek
Map by Mapping Specialists, Madison, Wisconsin
Picture research by Elizabeth Broadrup Lieberman

Published by Country Roads Press
A division of NTC/Contemporary Publishing Group, Inc.
4255 West Touhy Avenue, Lincolnwood (Chicago), Illinois 60646-1975 U.S.A.

Printed in the United States of America
International Standard Book Number: 1-56626-133-3

99 00 01 02 03 04 QP 19 18 17 16 15 14 13 12 11 10 9 8 7 6 5 4 3 2 1

For my girls, Kate and Dayne . . . again

Contents

Introduction ix

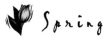 Spring

1 Call of the Wild *Peoria* 3
2 Lake Michigan Circle Tour
   Northeastern Illinois 7
3 Hemingway's Hometown *Oak Park* 15
4 Everything's OK at the Wyatt Earp Museum
   Monmouth 19
5 Land of Lincoln's Loopy Landmarks 21
6 Flower Fantasies 27
7 Abe's Birthday Bash *Springfield* 31
8 Museum Without Walls *Chicago Loop* 35
9 Where the "Real Baseball" Lives
   Dyersville, Iowa 41
10 Easter Awakenings *Bloomington* 45
11 From Treasures to Trinkets *Sandwich* 47
12 An Inn-Sider's Guide to Springtime Romance
   All Around Illinois 51
13 Lifestyles of the Rich and Famous *Vernon Hills* 55

 Summer

14 Great Times at Great America *Gurnee* 61
15 Riding the Rails to Weekend Adventure
   Far North, West, and South Suburban Chicago 65
16 State Fair Time *Springfield* 73
17 Home of the Man of Steel *Metropolis* 77
18 Prairie Primer *Morris* 79
19 Bearing Up Under the Sun *Platteville, Wisconsin* 83

20 Scottish Fling *Oak Brook* 85

21 Land of the Mound Builders *Collinsville* 89

22 Mozart Mania *Woodstock* 93

23 The Town That Time Forgot *Galena* 97

24 African American Legacies 103

25 Illinois State Parks 109

26 Corny Fun 117

27 Garfield Farm *Lafox* 121

28 Canoe Illini *Northern Illinois* 127

Fall

29 Apple Adventures *Wauconda* 137

30 Fall Color Caravan 141

31 Jackpot Journeys 147

32 Amish Sojourn *Arthur and Arcola* 153

33 The Great River Road
Along the Mississippi River 159

34 Up and Down on the Farm 165

35 Ghastly Gourds *Sycamore* 169

36 Shawnee Ramble *Southern Illinois* 171

37 Canal Capers *Lemont to La Salle* 177

38 An Honest Abe Thanksgiving *Petersburg* 183

39 An Oregon Outing 187

40 Stepping Back into Time *Elsah* 191

Winter

41 Road to Utopia *Bishop Hill* 197

42 Treasure Troves *Chicago* 201

43 Bogged Down in Winter *Ingleside* 205

44 Lights, Camera, Holiday Action
Findlay, Belleville, East Peoria 207

45 Where Eagles Dare *Rock Island* 211

46 Time Travels *Rockford* 215

47 Downhill Thrills 219

48 Tour-Riffic Chicago 223

49 A Final Yule Fling—with a French Accent
Ellis Grove 227

50 Chicago's Cultural Gems 229

51 Gonna Pump You Up *Gilman* 233

52 The Wright Stuff 237

Index 243

Introduction

CHICAGO IS MY KIND OF TOWN.

So is Galena. And Bishop Hill. Honest Abe's Springfield, too. And let's not forget the birthplace house of Ernest Hemingway. Or Frank Lloyd Wright's home and studio.

Michael Jordan.

Yep, there's lots to love about Illinois, especially if you've been born and bred in the Land of Lincoln, like this writer.

But, for me, Illinois is more than places to see and things to do. It's Midwest friendliness. Family values. And memories . . .

Like the McHenry County weekends at the farm of my aunt, where my brother Mark and I learned to drive in a beat-up old Pontiac. We motored that car all through the fields and woods of Aunt Esther and Uncle Bernie's farm, perfecting our Mario Andretti moves even though we were barely teenagers.

Of course, we wanted to show off our developing skills.

So we'd pull up to the farmhouse, beep the horn, and watch as our parents, and Grandma and Grandpa, filed out and piled into the car so we could take them on a grand tour of the cow pastures.

Then there's the little cottage at Wooster Lake that my family rented every summer when I was a kid. Days were filled with fishing expeditions led by Pa, followed by country cookout feasts prepared by Ma. And then there were weekend visits to the cottage by relatives, who seemed always willing to play in the Puhalas' annual summer softball classic.

(Since Grandpa played too, the rules were slightly altered. Catch the ball on a bounce or fly and you were out.)

And I'll never forget those frequent weekend rambles with Pa, spontaneous sunrise adventures where we'd gas up the car, point it in any direction, and explore until day's end. Our journeys took us to places like shrimp boats on the Mississippi River, hiking trails in southern Illinois amid the foothills of the Ozark Mountains, even to a reenactment of the famous "Gunfight at the OK Corral" at the Monmouth birthplace home of lawman Wyatt Earp.

We're trying to make Illinois come alive in the same way for our own children. Daughters Kate and Dayne have rubbed the nose of the Lincoln statue in Springfield, hoping for good luck. They've wolfed down barbecued corn, watched as state police patrolled on rollerblades, and sung along during a Barry Manilow concert at the State Fair. (Of course, they won't admit that to anyone anymore. Neither will I.)

And the kids have even kissed a mama llama during one of our weekend farm vacations.

I hope this book can guide your family to some of the same fun we're having in the Land of Lincoln. Maybe we'll even bump into you on one of your weekend adventures. That'd be real nice.

So hit the road with me—again. And enjoy Illinois!

Spring

1

Call of the Wild

PEORIA

BISON AND ELK WANDER ACROSS A VAST EXPANSE OF PRAIRIE grass. Bears and cougars cast their predatory eyes toward unsuspecting creatures from lairs in woodsy thickets and gnarled tree limbs. A pack of wolves wail their eerie howl from somewhere unseen.

"I can't believe this is real," gushes Kate, my then eight-year-old daughter. "It's like my history and science books came alive."

Kate's assessment is right on the money. The historic Illinois prairie comes alive at Wildlife Prairie Park, located about 10 miles west of Peoria. This unique 2,000-acre zoological park, a sister park of Chicago's world-renowned Brookfield Zoo, is a treasure trove of conservation education and family fun that may be the best-kept secret in Illinois.

It shouldn't be.

This is easily one of the nation's premier wildlife parks. Part theme park, part living-history museum, part conservation exhibit, Wildlife Prairie Park shows off the Illinois prairie as it appeared more than 200 years ago. It's home to more than 70 different living species on the endangered list and 300 endangered plants.

More than 10 miles of scenic hiking trails wind through lush forests and large enclosures, where animals that once inhabited the Illinois prairie seem to roam freely in their native habitat. Fences are designed to be inconspicuous, diminishing the perception of separation between the animals and their human visitors.

So inconspicuous that Dayne, our younger daughter, tells all her friends back home that she almost came "nose-to-nose" with a black bear who was lazing on a leaf-shrouded log near the perimeter of one of these enclosures. (In fact, the bear couldn't have gotten closer than six feet to her even if it tried; it didn't. It was sound asleep.)

"He sort of looks like Charlie Brown, but with bigger teeth," said Dayne. (Charlie Brown is our 100-pound chocolate Labrador retriever.)

"And he snores louder."

As we continue on the trails, the kids spot more animals. There are river otters, woodchucks, beavers, wild turkeys, skunks, raccoons, opossums, geese, coyotes, foxes, sandhill cranes—almost every historic species of the pioneer flatlands.

Including the badger.

"That guy looks really mean," said Dayne. Anyone who has ever encountered an enraged badger in the woods knows she's right.

Wildlife Prairie Park is the brainchild of William Rutherford, a Peoria attorney and environmentalist who once headed the Illinois Department of Conservation. In the late 1960s, Rutherford was working with Brookfield Zoo, putting together a central Illinois breeding farm and rest area to rehabilitate some of the zoo's endangered species; the grounds also would provide a refuge for the animals from the stress of the city.

When the zoo's management switched emphasis, Rutherford decided to build his own historic prairie park.

Today, more than 200,000 visitors annually come to this restored prairie and woodland to witness how native pioneer animals interact in the wild.

One of the park's more unusual exhibits is a three-quarter-acre eagle aerie, built at a cost of close to $100,000. A massive nylon rope net was dropped by helicopter over a nearly invisible framework 80 feet high and 250 feet square. Bald eagles fly through the treetops while beavers work in a pond and deer graze in the tall grass. (Only injured birds and those still on the mend are kept captive.)

Start your prairie wanderings at the stone-and-wood visitor center, where you can view natural history and conservation exhibits, as well as see an orientation slide show that backgrounds the park's wonders. Also note the schedule of special naturalist-led events taking place throughout the day; these can include everything from feeding time for bison and elk (when animals come right up to the prairie enclosure fence for their goodies) to nighttime "starlight walks" amid howling wolves and coyotes, an experience you'll never forget.

Then you can wind your way along self-guided walking trails that cut through prairie wilderness, a floodplain, even a replanted tallgrass prairie—the kind that covered more than 65 percent of Illinois only 200 years ago.

There's also a miniature 24-inch-gauge train, with about 9,000 feet of track, carrying visitors through a few park areas inaccessible by walking. Much of the ride is over reclaimed strip-mine land, so the train bobs over hillocks and gentle valleys left by that operation. (There is a small fee for train rides.)

Visit the park on Sunday for its popular "Brunch of the Prairie." Even the heartiest appetite will be satisfied by honey-glazed ham, baked chicken and/or fish, link sausage and bacon with scrambled eggs, biscuits with sausage gravy, fresh fruits and hot veggies, fresh-baked muffins, desserts, and beverages. Reservations are necessary.

Call of the Wild

And for a special treat, spend a night in the wild. You can choose the "Cabin on the Hill," located on a beautiful overlook of bison range, complete with a relaxing front-porch swing and playhouse for children.

But my girls can't wait to try out the park's train cabooses again. Each car comes with a jiggler switch to simulate a real train ride.

One last thing: Kate and Dayne still can't stop talking about the "Elkmobile." Make sure you get a chance to see it.

For More Information

For admission prices, seasonal hours, and special events, contact Wildlife Prairie Park, 3826 North Taylor Road, RR 2, Box 50, Peoria, IL 61615; (309) 676-0998.

Spring

2

Lake Michigan Circle Tour

NORTHEASTERN ILLINOIS

"HEY, PAPA! ARE WE THERE YET?"

"No, Dayne," I say to my daughter. "Just a few more minutes to Grandma's house."

One minute later.

"Hey, Papa! Are we there yet?" asks my daughter Kate.

"No, Katie, just a few more minutes."

One minute later.

"Hey, Papa! Are we there yet?" both of them chime up at the same time.

"Aaarrrrggggg!"

Only one thing saves Debbie and me from going stark raving bonkers from this endless interrogation: the beauty of the ride, which (depending on the route we choose) can include stretches of beautiful lakeshore, glimpses of sandy beaches, and peeps at the palatial estates of tony North Shore suburbs.

But we ride along only a small portion of what's been called Illinois's Lake Michigan Circle Tour. The entire journey, from the Illinois-Indiana border to the Wisconsin state line, is 74 miles long. It takes you on a fascinating north-south shoreline ramble that includes everything from the largest exposition center in America (McCormick Place) to the largest marina on the Great Lakes—with the world's tallest building thrown in the mix for extra entertainment.

Watch for special "Lake Michigan Circle Tour" signs posted along the way. Of course, all you've got to do is stay close to the lake, and you've got it made.

So hit the road and start your journey. Here are some of the highlights.

North Shore

Starting just north of Chicago on Sheridan Road in suburban Evanston, the Lake Michigan shoreline campus of Northwestern University may be one of the prettiest in the country. (And that's not just because I'm an alumnus of the school.) Tour the Lindheimer Astronomical Research Center, attend a big-name classical music concert at the Pick-Staiger Concert Hall, and see great works of art at the Mary and Leigh Block Gallery.

As early as 1673, the natural harbor of Grosse Pointe (just north of the university) lured French traders and missionaries (including Father Marquette) in their voyageur canoes to now Evanston's rocky beaches. But it wasn't until the wreck of the *Lady Elgin*, when 300 passengers perished in one of the Great Lakes' greatest maritime disasters, that a lighthouse was built on the bluff overlooking the harbor. You can tour the 1873 lighthouse, weekends from May through early October.

Then wander the downtown district, a chic tangle of upscale boutiques, art galleries, antique shops, and clothing stores (with some bookstores and other college-town businesses thrown in for good measure).

Continuing north to Wilmette, visit the magnificent Baha'i House of Worship. Set on a knoll with spectacular views of Lake Michigan, the domed-topped, nine-sided temple is surrounded by nine formal flower gardens, walkways, evergreens, and fountains. Its unique design (the hundreds of intricate stone panels, along with other architectural features, took 50 years to complete) has landed it on the National Register of Historic Places.

As Sheridan Road continues north, twisting and turning its way through ravines, woodlands, and the refined landscapes of Winnetka, Kenilworth, Glencoe, Highland Park, Lake Forest, and Lake Bluff, you quickly realize it's one of the most beautiful stretches of roadway in America. Architecture buffs are in for a treat, as these tony North Shore suburbs display some of the most elegant and impressive homes and mansions found anywhere.

Leaving the upper-crust suburbs but continuing north brings you to North Chicago. It's home to the Great Lakes Naval Training Center, America's largest sailor school. You can watch the military pageantry of graduation ceremonies here, which are open to the public; call for times and details.

Illinois Beach State Park in Zion encompasses seven miles of sandy beaches, a fabulous full-service lodge right on the lakeshore, and the last remaining sand dunes in Illinois. But it's the North Point Marina in Winthrop Harbor, just south of the Wisconsin state line, that gets more attention.

That's because this section of the Lake Michigan Circle Tour (LMCT) is known as the Coho Coast (a 12-mile stretch of northern Illinois's Lake Michigan shoreline). And it's home to one of the biggest charter fishing fleets on the Great Lakes. Angler wanna-bes should figure on spending about $250 for a half-day's coho adventure, which should cover costs for about six people.

The state-of-the-art North Point Marina, built for $51 million, is the largest marina on the Great Lakes, with 1,500 boat slips. Combine this with Waukegan's own 1,000-plus slips, and you've got a mecca for boaters and fishermen.

Lake Michigan Circle Tour

Chicago's Magnificent Mile

I'll match Chicago's magnificent Lake Shore Drive, skimming the crescent sand beaches that edge the shore while backed by the world's greatest skyline, against any comparable stretch of big-city road anywhere in the universe.

I guess Chicago is my kind of town.

Well, motoring up and down Lake Shore Drive is a good start to exploring the LMCT's Chicago connection. But if you've got time for only one Windy City dalliance, head for the Magnificent Mile.

Better known as North Michigan Avenue, it is one of the world's ritziest shopping meccas. Do the boutique crawl, taking you to stores like Tiffany's, Gucci, Neiman Marcus, Saks Fifth Avenue, Louis Vuitton, Bloomingdale's, and the huge complex of 100 shops built around an 8-story grand atrium in the 62-story Water Tower Place.

There are also snappier palaces of mass consumerism, like Sony's Gallery of Consumer Electronics, where all kinds of neat gadgets would put James Bond to shame. And then there's Nike Town, located right next door. Imagine a 68,000-square-foot shoe store, complete with its own basketball half-court so you can test out those Air Jordans and see if they make you hang in the air like Michael.

They don't.

On Oak Street, between Michigan Avenue and Rush, lie some of the most stylish boutiques in the world. Movie stars, singers, writers, and other glitterati descend on this stretch of commercial real estate that's said to roll up sales of more than $100 million each year.

Three other not-to-miss stops are the John Hancock Center, a 100-story office-commercial-residential structure that's only the third-tallest building in the city; across the street, the Fourth Presbyterian Church, a Gothic masterpiece with stained-glass windows and a small courtyard; and the Terra Museum of American Art, featuring some of the country's best painters and sculptors.

Walk farther south down Michigan Avenue to reach our "newspaper district." Actually, it's composed of just two buildings. But newspaper buffs will want to visit Tribune Tower, a 1925 Gothic Revival masterpiece, whose south side wall features copper etchings of famous newspaper headlines run by the *Chicago Tribune*; also look for pieces of stone said to be taken from famous buildings around the world.

Across the street, you can tour the editorial offices and massive printing plant of the *Tribune*'s scrappy rival, the *Chicago Sun-Times*. A glassed walkway in the *Sun-Times* Building is a favorite with kids, allowing close-up views of ink-stained pressmen preparing another day's latest edition.

Directly in front of the *Sun-Times* facilities is the Wrigley Building (yep, it's owned by the chewing gum family), topped by a massive clock tower copied from the Giralda Tower in Seville. Go through courtyard doors to reach the Plaza of the Americas, marked by flags of Western Hemisphere countries—it's a great place to people-watch, especially during a summertime lunch hour when the plaza fills with thousands of office workers. If you'd prefer to eat rather than watch other people eat, follow the plaza stairs down to the lower level; you'll arrive at the Billy Goat Tavern, a gritty city landmark made famous by the *Saturday Night Live*/John Belushi skit that made a catchphrase of "cheesbooger, cheesbooger, Pepsi, no Coke, cheeps."

At Michigan and Wacker, walk down the grand stairway of the Michigan Avenue Bridge to catch one of the city's cruise boats; the comfortable ships tour both the lakefront (offering postcard-perfect skyline vistas) and the Chicago River (where the narrow waterway is dwarfed by skyscrapers that seem to touch the heavens).

No weekend ramble on the Magnificent Mile would be complete without a ride to the top of Sears Tower, the world's tallest building. The behemoth, which cost $150 million and took three years to build, stands 110 stories tall: 1,454 feet worth of building and 1,707 feet to the top of its antenna.

It's worth the detour off the LMCT route into the Loop (at 233 South Wacker Drive) for a chance to board speedy elevators that take you to the skydeck observatory, exactly 103 stories above terra firma. They supposedly zip along at more than 20 miles per hour, reaching the observatory deck (1,353 feet) in about 55 seconds.

South Shore

The highlight of this LMCT segment is the Pullman Historic District. The country's largest-ever 19th-century planned industrial community sprawled over 600 acres, the brainchild of railroad magnate and inventor George Pullman, who created the coach car that bears his name.

Pullman built this company town for his employees beginning in 1880. In 1881, six families moved in; by 1886, the "town" counted 14,000 residents. Its golden age lasted until the depression of 1893; then came the bloody Pullman strike of 1894.

The economic downturn of 1893–94 had caused Pullman to lay off 3,000 workers, but he also cut wages of other employees 30 to 70 percent—while refusing to slash the rents paid to him by workers for company housing, even though his Pullman Palace Car Company declared 1894 undivided profits of $25 million.

Led by Eugene Debs, the American Railroad Union called for a strike against Pullman. Federal troops were called in by President Cleveland to keep order. Debs was arrested and jailed. But when Pullman fired a delegation of workers who came to him for strike negotiations, things got violent. And labor strife spread nationwide.

Pullman died three years later. Finally, the courts forced the company to sell its residential land holdings in 1898. "Pullman" reverted back to a "regular" Chicago neighborhood and slowly began to deteriorate.

Thanks to a spirited preservation effort, the Pullman neighborhood has been reborn as a historic district. Nearly 90 percent of its original buildings remain, from the tiny, brick-fronted row houses (complete with white front porches) built for unskilled workers to the grandiose Hotel Florence.

Start at the Historic Pullman Foundation offices, 11111 South Forestville; on weekends, you can walk across the street to the new visitor center. You'll see displays and photo exhibits that explain the history of this experimental utopia in urban planning. Individual guided walking tours are conducted on the first Sunday of each month, May through October. Or pick up a walking tour map of the area (50 cents at the Hotel Florence) and hit the bricks solo.

Here are a few highlights:

- The Greenstone Church, designed by Solon S. Berman (the architect responsible for 1,800 buildings in Pullman), gets its name from the green color of iron and magnesium contained in its serpentine limestone quarried in West Chester, Pennsylvania. Its distinctive styling, with rounded arches, a large spire, and massive masonry, is an interesting combination of Richardsonian Romanesque and country English Tudor. The church's beautiful rose window also has been restored.

- The Colonnade Apartments, which surround the oval of Market Hall at 112th and Champlain, are another curious architectural design. It has been written that "their

Lake Michigan Circle Tour

Romanesque arches seem more like the buildings of Savannah or New Orleans, while the rest of Pullman's housing resembles a New England mill town." Pullman's personal guests overnighted in these once-luxurious buildings while attending Chicago's 1893 World's Fair. After the event, Pullman rented them to his company's inventors, a group of workers he highly valued.

- Built in 1881, the Hotel Florence (named after Pullman's daughter) is a mass of Queen Anne–style gables and turrets. Originally, the four-story, 51-room hostelry even held a top-floor suite for the great man himself (although he usually holed up in his Prairie Avenue mansion). Today, you can enjoy Sunday brunch in handsome dining rooms, paneled in gleaming cherry wood and bathed in a kaleidoscope of colors from light shining through stained-glass windows.

For More Information

For more information and a list of overnight accommodations, contact the Illinois Bureau of Tourism, (800) 487-2446 or (800) 223-0121; the Chicago Office of Tourism, (312) 744-2400; the Chicago Department of Cultural Affairs, (312) 346-3278; Chicago Southland Convention and Visitors Bureau, (800) 873-9111; Lake County Convention and Visitors Bureau, (800) 525-3669; or the Historic Pullman Foundation, (773) 785-8181.

3

Hemingway's Hometown

OAK PARK

NOBODY REALLY KNOWS IF ERNEST HEMINGWAY, ONE OF THE greatest writers of the 20th century, ever said that Oak Park was "full of wide lawns and narrow minds." But he never wavered from his avowed hatred of the town and noted that he'd run away from it several times.

This could be just another instance of the macho myth-making that Hemingway, a masterful self-promoter, engaged in. And certainly his hometown doesn't hold any grudges—at least not anymore—because it has established a new Hemingway Museum, offers an "Explore Hemingway's Oak Park" walking tour, and celebrates "Fiesta de Hemingway" every July, complete with a "running of the bulls."

Any tour of Ernest Hemingway's Oak Park should start with his namesake museum at 200 North Oak Park Avenue. Part of the town's Arts Center, the museum offers all kinds of glimpses into the life of the author—who won the Pulitzer Prize in 1953 and the Nobel Prize for Literature in 1954.

For example, there's the first page of the first story he ever wrote (at age 12), titled "The Sea Vogue." You can see his first published story, "Judgment of Manitou," which appeared in *The Tabula* in 1916. There's one of his old typewriters. There's even a notebook, in which he announced his desire "to write and travel."

There's also other interesting stuff: pictures of Hemingway through the years, including his 1917 graduation photo from Oak Park and River Forest High School; family photos, especially those of his stern disciplinarian father, whose suicide haunted Hemingway; his childhood diary; spelling tests; his 1915 high school baseball season pass; and lots more.

Most fascinating might be the "Dear John" letter (or should I say, "Dear Ernest") from Agnes Von Kurowsky, the nurse who cared for Hemingway when he suffered serious mortar shell wounds in Italy as an ambulance driver for the Red Cross during World War I; of course, any Hemingway fan knows that Von Kurowsky became the model for "Catherine Barkley," the nurse in his autobiographical novel *A Farewell to Arms*.

You also can watch a six-minute video about the author's Oak Park high school years. And a new exhibit area features an extensive videotape collection of Hollywood films based on Hemingway material. Call (708) 524-5383.

I've yet to tell you that Hemingway was born on July 21, 1899, because I wanted to save this tidbit of information until we discussed his birthplace house, located at 339 North Oak Park Avenue. His physician father announced the birth of Ernest, the second of six children, by wildly blowing his cornet on the wraparound porch of the home, which is being restored.

In fact, the house just opened as a museum in 1993, being deconverted from a two-flat. Tours of the 1890s Queen Anne–style house even take you to the room in which Hemingway was born. Call (708) 445-3070.

You can obtain a self-guided walking tour map of other Hemingway landmarks from the Oak Park Visitors Center, 158 Forest Avenue, (708) 848-1500. The tour includes:

- The Hemingway "Interim House," 161 North Grove Avenue, which the family rented from 1905 to 1906 while their new home on Kenilworth Avenue was being constructed. It's now a private house.

- Hemingway's Boyhood Home, 600 North Kenilworth Avenue, where his family lived until 1936. Young Ernest occupied the center bedroom on the third floor facing Iowa Street. There was a 30- by 30-foot music room where his mother gave music lessons; when it was empty, Ernest practiced boxing there. It's currently divided into three private apartments.

Hemingway attended Holmes Elementary School (500 North Kenilworth Avenue) and Oak Park and River Forest High School (201 North Scoville Avenue); the latter's Hemingway Room, with its beamed-ceiling construction, is now being restored. Call (708) 383-0700.

You can find Hemingway's name inscribed on the Oak Park and River Forest War Memorial in Scoville Park. The World War I monument honors the memory of the town's 56 dead and 2,400 who served in that conflict. The writer's name is on the southeast side of the base.

And the Oak Park Public Library, 834 Lake Street, houses an extensive Hemingway collection. In 1953, the writer sent a letter here expressing his appreciation for "how much I owe the library and how much it meant to me." He even enclosed a $100 check to cover any unpaid overdue book fines!

Hemingway lived in Oak Park until the spring of 1917. Soon after high school graduation, he became a cub reporter for the *Kansas City Star*.

Whatever Hemingway really thought of the Chicago suburb where he was born, one thing is certain: his Oak Park experiences, both in school and as a part of this community, had a profound influence on his writings.

For More Information

For more Oak Park/Ernest Hemingway information, contact the Ernest Hemingway Foundation of Oak Park, P.O. Box 2222, Oak Park, IL 60303; (708) 848-2222. This not-for-profit organization sponsors lectures, tours, films, and the annual "Fiesta de Hemingway," a week-long celebration in July that includes a re-creation of Pamplona's famed "running of the bulls."

4

Everything's OK at the Wyatt Earp Museum

MONMOUTH

ALTHOUGH WYATT EARP WAS A LAWMAN FOR ONLY 5 OF his 80 years, more than 25 movies have been made of his exploits as one of the legendary peacemakers in the Old West.

And his "Gunfight at the OK Corral," a notorious 15-second shoot-out pitting Wyatt, brothers Virgil and Morgan, and Doc Holliday against cattle rustlers in Tombstone, Arizona Territory, on October 26, 1881, may be the most celebrated "shoot-'em-up" of the era.

So it's only natural that his hometown, tiny Monmouth in western Illinois, salutes its favorite son with a grand party throughout the year. The year's first Wyatt fest is a birthday celebration, held annually in mid-March. Born on March 19, 1848, in the modest Monmouth house of his Aunt Lizzie, Wyatt lived in town for six years on three different occasions, leaving Monmouth for good in 1869.

His birthplace home, 406 South Third Street, now grandly called the Historic House Museum, is open for tours during the birthday bash. The two-story, Greek Revival–style building, built in 1842, is furnished in four "time periods" stretching from 1840 to 1880.

An interesting wrinkle: your guided tour might even be led by Earp cousins, several of whom still live in Monmouth.

Besides Earp, family photos, papers, books, and furniture, news stories, and other memorabilia trace Wyatt's lawman career. Duplicates of his famous long-barreled guns also are on display. There is an admission fee for tour tickets.

But before you head to Wyatt's house, you'll want to attend a special buffet lunch at a local restaurant (the location sometimes changes, so check before you go), which features an Earp look-alike contest, and a slide show depicting Earp's career as a deputy U.S. marshal. Again, there is an admission charge.

You also can pick up a free Wyatt Earp tour map at the birthplace house museum. Townie sights along the way include the Earp Monument at North Eleventh Street, the spot where Earp hid from Indians with his brothers as a kid; and the Pioneer Cemetery on North Sixth Street, where his grandparents are buried.

Make sure you experience a slice of the Old West by climbing aboard an authentically reproduced stagecoach of the Earp era. It carries dudes and dudettes on 15-minute-long rides through town, including a run past Earp's house. There is a fee for rides.

Of course, if you go to the Earp House during the summer, especially during Wild West Days in August and a certain date in October, you might even catch a reenactment of the Gunfight at the OK Corral. Make sure you call ahead for these dates—and smile when you say that, pardner.

FOR MORE INFORMATION

The Wyatt Earp House and Museum is open from Memorial Day through Labor Day. For more information, contact the Wyatt Earp House, 406 South Third Street, Monmouth, IL 61462; (309) 734-6419.

5

Land of Lincoln's Loopy Landmarks

"THIS IS A JOKE, RIGHT, PAPA?" MY THEN FOUR-YEAR-OLD daughter, Dayne, asked me as we stood in front of a truly weird Americana shrine.

The object of her amazement was a two-story outhouse standing in Gays (population 250), located about 20 miles southwest of Arcola.

It dates back to the 1880s, built to be used by two second-story apartments of a general store long since demolished. The outhouse's interior walls are offset so waste can drain from the second story to the ground, out of range and (hopefully) downwind of others.

Locals call it the "skyscrapper."

Wild, weird, wacky, wonderful—these are just a few of the adjectives used to describe Illinois's unusual little landmarks and museums, like the second-story bathroom in Gays. Here's a list pinpointing other "best bets" for a summer of offbeat weekend touring delights.

And remember, when visiting tiny museums in out-of-the-way locations, it's especially important that you call ahead to confirm hours of operation and admission fees (if any).

French Embassy Bowling Restaurant How about a great French gourmet dinner, followed by a couple lines of bowling? That's on the menu at the French Embassy Bowling Restaurant in Arcola. Don't get the wrong idea. Chef Jean-Louis Ledent, who came to the United States from Belgium in 1987, offers quite good French cuisine at his unusual establishment. Consider choices like quail with onions and bacon; sautéed lamb with garlic, white Bordeaux sauce, and artichoke hearts; and bouillabaisse, which must be ordered a full week in advance. Even the wine list is more than satisfactory, including a selection of Alsatian vintages. Once finished, you can work off that heavy French meal by pushing yourself away from the table, walking over to the lanes, and bowling a few lines. Call (217) 268-3331.

Ronald Reagan Boyhood Home 816 South Hennepin Avenue (off Main Street), Dixon. Take a guided tour through the humble house where Ronnie lived from 1920 to 1923. When my daughter Kate, then four, wandered into the ex-president's bedroom and tossed around a football that was on display, I was mortified, but our guide assured us that Reagan would not mind that minor indiscretion one bit. Call (815) 288-3404.

Whistling Wings 113 Washington Street, Hanover. Have a quacking-good time at the largest mallard hatchery in the world, producing more than 200,000 ducks annually. If all those sweet duckie eyes don't capture your heart, you can purchase take-home goodies like smoked mallards, quail, pheasant, and other wild game. Call (815) 591-3512.

Original Mineral Springs Hotel and Bath House 506 Hanover Street, Okawville. OK, so this isn't really a museum. But this is the only section of the book where I could mention that Illinois has its own natural mineral springs, going strong since Native Americans introduced the white man to them in 1867. Today, you can soak in a natural mineral bath whose waters once were thought to soothe all kinds of maladies, or even get a massage. Call (618) 243-5458.

Elephant's Graveyard See the elephant's graveyard in Oquawka, about 30 miles west of Galesburg. It's the final resting place for Norma Jean, a 6,500-pound pachyderm. The circus star was 30 years old when struck by a lightning bolt; her handler was tossed more than 30 feet by the energy flash. A monument marks her final resting place. It took a heavy tractor equipped with thick metal chains to place Norma Jean into her final resting place—a grave that had to be dug more than 12 feet into the ground.

Historic Barn Tours 118 Randolph, Macomb. Here's one "museum" that makes visitors hit the road to view the exhibits. Actually, you can obtain a free brochure outlining three self-guided historic barn tours, which include an unusual "turn-around" barn as well as an impressive "cross-gable." Call (309) 833-1315.

Warren Cheese Plant 415 Jefferson Street, Warren. If you don't know jack, you'll become a cheese whiz by watching it being made while learning secrets that created Apple Jack and other award-winning string cheeses. Call (815) 745-2627.

M and M Exotic Animal Walk-Through Park State 4, Metropolis. Yep, you can take a leisurely stroll among lions, llamas, bears, and other animals at this secluded reserve near the heart of Shawnee National Forest. Call (618) 524-7333.

Mari-Mann Herb Farm at the north end of St. Louis Bridge Road, Decatur. Snack on herbal hors d'oeuvres, geranium cakes, and spiced teas while walking through formal gardens, wildflower fields, and deer trails. Call (217) 429-1404.

Woodland Palace on State 34 in Francis Park, Kewanee. Years ahead of its time, this home built by Frederick Francis more than a century ago features "disappearing" doors and windows, an air-cooling system, radiant-heat deflectors, and running water—all without benefit of electricity. Call (309) 852-0511.

Rock Island Arsenal Arsenal Island, Rock Island. One of the largest arsenals in the world, built in 1833, is located in the middle of the Mississippi River. Its museum features all kinds of martial displays, from suits of armor and cavalry swords to rifles used by Union troops in the Civil War. You'll also see a replica of the old Fort Armstrong blockhouse and a Confederate Soldier Cemetery. Call (309) 793-1604.

Ingram's Log Cabin Village State 2, Kinmundy. Located just north of town, the village features pre–Civil War log structures moved here from all over southern Illinois. You'll find an apothecary shop, a grocer's store, a cobbler's shop, a post office, and a church. Call (618) 547-7123 or (618) 547-3241.

Spring

Vinegar Hill Historic Lead Mine and Museum 8885 North Three Pines Road, Galena. In the "town that time forgot," fortunes were made in mining lead. This Galena operation dates to the 1870s and offers underground mine tours through one of its shallow shafts. Then browse through a museum filled with lead samples from the mine, miners' tools and equipment, and other mining-era artifacts. Call (815) 777-0855.

Geneseo Historical Museum 212 South State Street, Geneseo. The main claim to fame here is what's hyped as the "largest arrowhead and Indian exhibit" in Illinois. You also can step into a turn-of-the-century country store or laze in a fully furnished Victorian parlor. Call (309) 944-3043.

The Lincoln Douglas Valentine Museum 101 North Fourth Street, Quincy. If you're looking for Valentine's Day card ideas, this is the right place for you. Hundreds of antique and unusual valentines are on display. Call (217) 224-3355.

Beer Nuts, Inc. 103 North Robinson Street, Bloomington. You guessed it! This is the place where those delicious little nuts are manufactured. At the plant's outlet store, you'll discover that they hit the market in 1930 as "Virginia Redskins" peanuts. You also can see a video showing how the peanuts are made. And I dare you to leave without buying some of these tasty snacks. Call (309) 827-8580.

Oliver P. Parks Telephone Museum 529 South Seventh Street, Springfield. Dial up lots of fun at this museum named for a longtime employee of the Bell Telephone Company whose collection consists of more than a hundred antique telephones. (Can you believe it? There's no working phone on the premises!)

Monastery Museum 110 South Garrett Street, Teutopolis. You'll see more than 2,000 artifacts of the Franciscan fathers, from the simple dishes they used to a Bible collection that includes "The Word" in 12 languages. Call (217) 857-3328.

For More Information

For more information about touring Illinois, contact the Illinois Bureau of Tourism, (800) 223-0121.

6

Flower Fantasies

NOW THAT SPRING IS HERE, ALL IT'LL TAKE IS A LITTLE cooperation from Mother Nature before wildflowers, formal gardens, and blossom festivals sprout a kaleidoscope of blooming colors. From lilac-filled islands to botanical reserves, blossoming flowers herald the coming of an Illinois summer in spectacular fashion. Just think of the entire region as your own personal "backyard" and explore wildflower-dotted prairie in Goose Lake, lilac-lined roads in Lombard, breathtaking rose gardens surrounding a historic Urbana estate—or your own favorite flower paradise.

So if you want to stop and smell the roses, or any other kind of spring blossom, here are some of the Land of Lincoln's most impressive flower hot spots.

Formal Gardens

At Robert Allerton Park in Monticello, visitors get both a spectacular formal flower garden and an outdoor art museum. The 1,500-acre estate, with its European flavor and classical overtones, offers manicured flower beds, reflecting ponds, wildflower meadows, wooded preserves, and a wildlife sanctuary.

A bonus is more than a hundred stately statues, including a representation of the "Charioteers of Delphi." And while Carl Mille's statue "The Sun Singer" has come to characterize the park for many visitors, other favorites are the 22 blue Chinese Fu Dogs that form a double line against a backdrop of white fir trees. There's also an art deco sunken garden lined with statues of 12 musical figures, site of numerous weddings, and lily, chrysanthemum, and peony gardens. Admission is free; call (217) 762-2721.

Flower Preserves

Chicago Botanic Garden Perhaps my favorite close-to-home nature getaway is the Chicago Botanic Garden in Glencoe. Blossom gardens, formal gardens, wildflower prairie gardens, and home demonstration gardens are sprawled along more than 300 acres of prime North Shore property. The Puhala family loves to wander through the lush rose garden, with its endless variety of fragrant buds. Another treat is a stunning three-island Japanese garden that includes a Zen meditation garden that'll get your yin and yang balanced in no time. There's even a unique sensory garden for the visually impaired.

Other highlights are the Heritage Garden, modeled after the first botanic garden in Padua, Italy, and Waterfall Garden, whose footpath leads to a 45-foot-tall waterfall. You don't even have to walk or drive through the preserve to discover its beauty; just sign up for a half-hour tram tour that'll showcase all the loveliness.

Some of our favorite times to visit: spring planting and harvest season, when vegetable demonstration gardens are exploding with ideas or crops; and winter, when you can bundle up under a buffalo blanket inside a horse-drawn sleigh and glide over a wonderland of snowy flatlands. Other annual events include a spring Japanese festival, summer carillon concerts, and a winter orchard display. Call (847) 835-5440.

Morton Arboretum In Lisle, the Morton Arboretum is filled with all kinds of flowery excess. However, this unique 1,500-acre conservatory of plants offers not only blooming surprises, but also an astonishing number and variety of trees. Even the rare ginkgo tree can be found here. And you can enjoy all this natural beauty in a trekkers' paradise, thanks to the preserve's more than 25 miles of walking and driving trails. Especially noteworthy is the Illinois Tree Trail Loop #1. Best times to come: springtime for blossoming magnolias and wildflowers; lilacs in May; summer prairie flowers; and peak autumn colors in mid- to late October. Call (630) 968-0074.

Wildflowers

Goose Lake Prairie State Natural Area in Morris is one of the largest tracts of tallgrass prairie left in North America and a reminder of the environment that greeted settlers on their way through here in pioneer times. While its grasses, once reaching as high as a horse's shoulder, seem to endlessly sway in the wind, the park's wildflowers are a prime attraction during the spring season.

Prairie meadows explode in a cacophony of bluebells, black-eyed susans, and tall sunflowers; marked trails let you hike for miles enveloped by nature's beauty. Admission is free; call (815) 942-2899.

Flower Fantasies

Flower Festivals

Lilac Time Lombard's world-famous Lilac Time, a two-week festival in early May, showcases more than 1,200 lilacs and 40,000 tulips in Lilacia Park. Included in the nine-acre spread are more than 200 varieties of lilacs; 50 kinds of tulips; perennials and annuals; and an herb garden.

Lilacs were planted by a Civil War veteran officer, who owned the estate that's now a park; he purchased his lilac plants directly from LeMoine Gardens in France more than a hundred years ago. The fest also offers outdoor concerts, kids' activities, an art show, a lilac parade, and more. There is a nominal Lilacia Park admission fee. Call the park at (630) 953-6000. For Lilac Time information, call (630) 629-3799.

Spring

Gladioulus Festival Let's not forget the glad times in Momence, when gladioli galore, in acre after acre of swaying fields, bloom in bright reds, pale yellows, and unusual pastel hues. These tall-stemmed perennials are at their best during the town's Gladiolus Festival, held annually in mid-August. Why gladioli in Momence? Seems that cultivation began earnestly in 1909 when a local pickle factory owner started raising the flowers in his own backyard. Then things just naturally blossomed.

The town has been saluting its gladiolus connection since 1938. Its festival features a flower show and display, a carnival and midway, a huge parade with gladioli-laden floats, and more. If you still haven't gotten your gladiolus fix, point your car south of Momence on State 1 and drive the St. Ann township roads. Just east of the highway, you'll see nearly 500 acres of fabulous gladiolus blossoms—they usually last from mid-July through mid-September. And visit one of several major area gladiolus growers, whose flower farms produce more than 60 gladiolus varieties; you can buy some take-home flowers at the farms' flower sheds. Call (815) 472-4620.

7

Abe's Birthday Bash

SPRINGFIELD

IT IS SAID THAT SPRINGFIELD, NOTHING MORE THAN "A POINT in the prairie near Spring Creek" when founded in 1821, became the Illinois state capital 16 years later "due in large part to the political maneuverings of a young politician named Abraham Lincoln."

So it's fitting that the city annually celebrates Honest Abe's birthday with everything from guided tours of his restored Springfield home and patriotic parades to scholarly seminars and book discussions exploring even the most intimate details of the 16th president's life.

There are also plenty of Lincoln sites to visit, including his law office, the Old State Capitol, and the elaborate monument marking his tomb at Oak Ridge Cemetery.

You can even take a look at Abe's personal ledger, in which he kept track of his monthly mortgage payments and grocery bills.

For a good overview of Lincoln's Springfield, a great starting point is the Lincoln Home National Historic Site at 8th and Jackson. Part of a four-block historic neighborhood that still looks much as it did in the 1850s, the handsome 1839 Quakerbrown house was the only home Abe ever owned.

It's been authentically restored with many items belonging to the Lincoln household, and it reproduces exterior and interior colors, wallpapers, and carpets as the family knew them.

Tour tickets are free, distributed at the nearby visitor center (426 South Seventh Street) on a first-come, first-served basis each day; each ticket indicates a specific tour time. Be sure to arrive early; waiting time can range from 15 minutes to several hours. Visitor center hours are daily 8:30 A.M. to 5:00 P.M. Call (217) 492-4150.

The Lincoln-Herndon Law Offices State Historic Site, at 6th and Adams, is where Abe practiced his craft from 1843 until he left in 1861 for Washington, D.C., and his presidency. Tours of the restored offices give you a glimpse into legal practices of 1850s Springfield. Hours are 9:00 A.M. to 5:00 P.M.; call (217) 785-7289.

Lincoln gave his famous "House Divided" speech in the Old State Capitol, now a state historic site off the downtown mall. Rooms are furnished in 1840–1860 period pieces; you can visit the Supreme Court chambers, where Abe tried more than 200 cases, and view an original copy of the Gettysburg Address, displayed in the building's rotunda room. Hours are 9:00 A.M. to 5:00 P.M.; call (217) 785-7961.

Check the visiting hours of three lesser-known Lincoln sites: the family pew at the First Presbyterian Church, 7th and Capitol, which also contains beautiful stained-glass windows, (217) 528-4311; his personal ledger, which kept accounts of all Lincoln family bills, on display at Bank One, 6th and Washington, (217) 525-9600; and the Great Western Depot, the rail station where Lincoln departed Springfield for his uncertain future as president. It offers restored waiting rooms (one for tobacco-spitting men only) and a slide show re-creating Lincoln's 12-day journey to his inauguration, (217) 544-8695.

If it's special events you're after, Abe's annual birthday weekend celebration begins Saturday morning at the Lincoln Tomb State Historic Site in Oak Ridge Cemetery with an Annual National Pilgrimage. Wreaths are placed in the Burial Chamber and patriotic songs are performed.

After the ceremonies, go inside the chamber; but be sure to rub the nose of the bronze head of Lincoln standing at the tomb entrance, said to bring good luck. A winding corridor flanked by more Lincoln sculptures leads to the solemn Burial Chamber, where a seven-ton block of red granite marks Abe's final resting place—which is actually 30 inches behind the marker and 10 feet below the surface of the floor.

Also climb the steps of the memorial to the second terrace level, where you can get a closer look at the site's 117-foot-tall obelisk and massive carved statues representing Civil War fighting forces. Cemetery hours are daily 9:00 A.M. to 5:00 P.M.; call (217) 782-2717.

Other annual Lincoln birthday weekend events:

- The Lincoln Home offers Lincoln Heritage Lectures, mornings at the visitor center. In the past, noted Lincoln scholars have spoken on everything from Honest Abe's presidential mail and the tragic life of Mary Lincoln to the posthumous Lincoln in cartoon art. Admission is free.

- In the Old State Capitol's Hall of Representatives, the Annual Abraham Lincoln Symposium is held. Prominent historians discuss issues like "New Directions in Lincoln Studies," including the recent controversy over the use of Lincoln's DNA to determine whether the 16th president suffered from Marfan's syndrome, and recent Lincoln forgeries. Admission is free.

- The Abraham Lincoln Association Banquet, a grand evening affair usually held at the Springfield Renaissance Hotel Ballroom, features all kinds of special fun. One year, actor Sam Waterston, star of the former Broadway show "Abe Lincoln in Illinois," performed a selection of Lincoln's most famous speeches. Admission is charged; advance reservations are necessary.

- On Sunday morning, go back to Lincoln's Tomb at Oak Ridge Cemetery for the Annual Pilgrimage of the Veter-

Abe's Birthday Bash

ans of Foreign Wars. A grand parade of flags proceeds from the cemetery entrance to the front of the tomb. It is immediately followed by a eulogy service that includes a flag display, patriotic songs, uniformed soldiers, and a 21-gun salute.

Of course, any time of year is a great time to visit Lincoln sites. And you can use Springfield as the starting point to travel the Lincoln Trail, which includes the New Salem State Historic Site (a log cabin village where he lived for six years) in Petersburg; the Mt. Pulaski Courthouse, where Abe appeared before the bench; the town of Lincoln, where a giant watermelon-slice statue commemorates the statesman for his August 27, 1853, christening of the "new community" (town lots were sold to begin a new city) with the juice of a watermelon; the Postville Courthouse, Decatur, where a statue marks the spot of Abe's first public speech.

And other Lincoln sites wander into Indiana (where he lived for 14 years) and Kentucky (tour his birthplace log cabin).

FOR MORE INFORMATION

Springfield is about 190 miles south of Chicago. For more information about annual Lincoln Birthday weekend activities or Lincoln historic sites, contact the Springfield Convention and Visitors Bureau, (800) 545-7300 or (217) 789-2360. A good book pinpointing Lincoln historic sites and history is *In Lincoln's Footsteps* by Don Davenport (Prairie Oak Press, Madison, WI).

8

Museum Without Walls

CHICAGO LOOP

WALKING AROUND CHICAGO'S LOOP IS LIKE STROLLING through a "museum without walls," where seemingly on every corner or in every courtyard you're likely to encounter major works by some of the world's most famous artists.

Pablo Picasso, Claes Oldenburg, Joan Miró, Jean Dubuffet, Augustus Saint Gaudens, Lorado Taft—these are just some of the artistic visionaries whose creations are on outdoor display rather than sitting in musty museums.

In fact, public art in Chicago, encompassing all the forms of visual art imaginable, has been characterized as "one of the finest collections of contemporary works in the world."

All it takes to enjoy it is a good pair of walking shoes (and, hopefully, good weather). So here's a guide to some of the Loop's most impressive public artworks.

"The Picasso" What the Eiffel Tower is to Paris, "The Picasso" has become to Chicago. Installed on the plaza grounds of the Richard J. Daley Civic Center in 1967, the untitled contemporary monument inspired a cultural renaissance in downtown Chicagoland and "evoked a new emphasis on private and public investment in public art."

Not that it didn't cause a lot of controversy when it was unveiled. Its 50-foot-high, three-dimensional abstract design, constructed of Cor-Ten steel, angered many people who expected a more traditional artwork.

What is it? A giant bird with massive wings? The profile of the late mayor himself? Picasso never told. But one familiar with his work can see a woman's head and face that combines front and side views at the same time, creating a "double-exposure" effect, thus provoking the observer to see it in a new way every time (and from many perspectives). Heck, even the sculpture itself has changed, its steel skin acquiring a permanent patina through a rusting process that transformed its color from gray to a deep brown. Located at 50 West Washington Street.

"Batcolumn" Ten years after "The Picasso," another gargantuan sculpture appeared in what's now called the Harold Washington Social Security Administration Building Plaza. Many guessed that it was the glorified bat of Ernie Banks, a Hall of Fame baseball player for the city's ever-hapless Chicago Cubs.

But Claes Oldenburg's "Batcolumn" is "making a perpendicular to the magnificent horizontal" of the Chicago panorama.

Another Cor-Ten steel design, it's a 100-foot-tall monument that art critics say "combines a humorous and irreverent attitude toward popular objects with meticulous construction details and handling of scale and proportion." Okay, but is it saluting America's game of baseball or the steel industry? Located at 600 West Madison.

"The Four Seasons" One of my favorite works remains Marc Chagall's "The Four Seasons," a massive monolith (70 by 14 by 10 feet) adorned with hand-chipped stone and glass fragments resting at the First National Plaza. Characterized by Chagall's usual paintings (images of flowers, birds, fish, suns, lovers, etc.), the six pastel-hued scenes are composed of thousands of tiny chips of more than 250 colors.

Chagall said of his architectural mosaic, "The seasons represent human life, both physical and spiritual, at its different ages." In fact, the artist even included a rendition of the fabulous Chicago skyline in his work. Located at Dearborn and Monroe.

"The Town Ho's Story"   Talk about art generating controversy. Frank Stella's "The Town Ho's Story," sitting in front of the Ralph H. Metcalfe Federal Building, raised eyebrows on many levels.

Some didn't like its name (which refers to a chapter in Melville's classic *Moby Dick*, where a sailor uses "both mind and fist to resist mistreatment"). Others just plain didn't like it. And a few called it a pile of junk.

The unusual piece is an 18-foot-high amalgam composed of several smaller sculptures made of structural steel, stainless steel, and aluminum, then covered with molten aluminum to achieve a cohesive shape. It weighs in at over 13,000 pounds. And it evokes Stella's abstract paintings.

In the words of the artist, it "embodies similar energies in aluminum and steel, using the power of abstraction to compress into one expansive space the gleaming, combative essence of a literary work and an American city."

Of course. Located at 77 West Jackson Boulevard.

"Reading Cones"   Want to see Chicago's own Stonehenge? In Grant Park sits "Reading Cones" by Richard Serra, and it's one of the city's best Minimalist works. Two austere, solid steel cupped walls sit like an ancient monument in the midst of downtown Chicago's biggest public park. There's a slight opening in between the walls, just large enough so that one person can squeeze through at a time. This isolated passage is designed to overwhelm the viewer with a feeling of supernatural force that could prevent him/her from leaving the space. At least that's what some art critics say. Located in Grant Park on Monroe Street between Columbus Drive and Lake Shore Drive.

"Flamingo" Alexander Calder's "Flamingo" looks like a massive metal bird flapping its steel-beamed wings within the steel-and-glass gridiron of skyscrapers that surround the Federal Center Plaza. The 53-foot-tall, vermilion-colored construction is a dramatic, fluid sculpture that, according to Calder, he simply made up as he went along in the creative process. Despite its name, Calder insists that it is purely an abstract work; he named it "Flamingo" because "it was sort of pink and has a long neck." Located at Dearborn and Adams Streets.

Joan Miró Radiating the "mystical force of a great Earth Mother," Joan Miró's 39-foot-tall creation in the Brunswick Building Plaza cost $500,000 to build. Made of steel, wire mesh, concrete, bronze, and ceramic tiles, it was cast in the artist's hometown of Barcelona, then finished here. The fully rounded form has definite female likenesses, similar to earlier Miró paintings and ceramics. Located at 69 West Washington Street.

"Monument with Standing Beast" Large-scale sculpture in a brutal urban realm has always been a favorite medium for Jean Dubuffet. His "Monument with Standing Beast," resting in the James R. Thompson Center Plaza, is a testament to this notion. The 29-foot-tall fiberglass work is a primitive shape of four interrelated elements that the artist described as "drawing which extends into space." From afar, it looks like the cardboard cutouts of the Jolly Green Giant's kid. Located at 100 West Randolph Street.

"Freeform" If Abstract Expressionism is for you, don't miss Richard Hunt's "Freeform," erected as an exterior facade on the Illinois State Office Building. The massive, modernistic skyscraper, itself an object of architectural and artistic controversy, dwarfs Hunt's work. But do not be deceived; the stainless steel "biomorphic form" (it looks like a big octopus) measures 26 by 35 by 2 feet—almost two-and-a-half stories high.

It is supposed to represent an individual's pursuit of his/her own unique form of expression, perfect for a government building where the legal apparati to protect individual rights and freedoms reside. Located at 160 North LaSalle Street.

"Large Interior Form" Henry Moore's "Large Interior Form" stands outside in the Stanley McCormick Memorial Court of the Art Institute of Chicago. The 16.5-foot-tall bronze is a three-dimensional representation of the human figure. Somebody once said it looked like a warped Oscar statue with three holes in it; the artist said he tried to create "organism[s] that must be complete in themselves, of having grown organically created by pressure from within." Huh? Located off Michigan Avenue near Monroe Street.

For More Information

For more information on Chicago's outdoor art (including public art guide books and walking tours), contact the Chicago Office of Tourism, Department of Cultural Affairs, Public Art Program, (312) 346-3278; for other Chicago information, call (312) 744-2400.

9

Where the "Real Baseball" Lives

DYERSVILLE, IOWA

A FEW YEARS AGO DURING MY ANNUAL "SPRING TRAINING" visit to the *Field of Dreams* cornfield stadium in this tiny northeastern Iowa town just across the Illinois border, I finished running the base paths with my two baseball-crazy daughters and wandered over to a wooden box containing vials of dirt from this dream diamond.

I chose one labeled "Left Field," the place where those ghost ballplayers materialized out of tall stands of corn in Kevin Costner's 1989 movie about a farmer who plows up his fields and carves out a ballpark because a voice told him to make one.

"If you build it, he will come," said the disembodied whisper in the flick.

Well, Shoeless Joe Jackson, a legendary player thrown out of baseball for his alleged part in the Black Sox Scandal of 1919 (when the White Sox "threw" the World Series to the Cincinnati Reds), along with his ball-playing friends, did show up in the movie.

I have visited the field several times since the movie's release. Now my wife was with me.

"You're buying dirt?" she asked.

"It's not just dirt," I answered. "It's . . . well, kind of hard to explain."

"Try," she said. "Because I can't imagine a container of dirt sitting on the top of your dresser in our bedroom."

So I explained how the movie (and the field) had brought back memories of all the hours I'd played ball throughout my life—and what those memories still mean to me.

I remember how proud I was to play my first Little League game at Churchill Field in the old neighborhood, clothed in a real baseball uniform for the first time.

It helped me remember my first at bat in organized ball, a triple to right-center that could've been a home run if I'd remembered in my excitement to slide into home plate. So the next time up, I blasted one over the railroad viaduct, an automatic homer—and didn't have to worry about sliding at all.

I thought of moving up to Pony League, Babe Ruth, high school, and college, and how I developed into a pretty good breaking ball pitcher. The dirt also reminds me about my tryouts with the Houston Astros and Kansas City Royals.

And my look-see by the Cincinnati Reds, a real disaster.

After being invited to tryout camp, the Cincy coach led me out to the pitcher's mound and bellowed, "Let me see your smoke, son!"

"I'm a location pitcher, lots of off-speed stuff," I told him.

"Just smoke it," he answered.

"First let me show you my breaking stuff. I'm sure that's why I'm here."

He kind of squinted at me and spit out a brown stream of tobacco juice.

"Son, I don't care if your curveball can turn the corner, circle the block, and jump back into your pocket. If you ain't got heat, that's that."

My fastest fastball was clocked at about 80 mph.

"Next," the coach shouted.

So I explained all of this to my wife, and more. About how my Pa, after working hard 10 hours every day, came home and even before dinner spent some time hitting fly balls and grounders to me at the neighborhood park. Or how my Ma timed dinners to fall between games at our local ball field; she'd look out the attic window of our Chicago six-flat, and I'd signal the inning to her.

And I explained how I felt the first time I brought our girls to this park, how this had been their first taste of real baseball. About how they shouted and squealed with delight as they ran and slid into the bases. About how they'd pretend that Harry Carey would announce their name before they'd grab a bat and step into the box.

About how a father had begun passing down the love of a little kids' game to his daughters.

"All right," my wife said, finally convinced. "Just put the dirt in the drawer when company comes over, OK?"

But these are precisely the kinds of memories stirred up by this little ball field, which was almost plowed under after filming on the movie wrapped up. However, it was saved by Betty Boeckenstedt, sister of one of the field's co-owners, who thought the field "looked so nice" that the "family might come play ball out there."

The family did come—baseball's family, some from as far away as Japan and Australia—to this little speck of cornfield in Iowa. Sometimes as many as 3,000 on a Sunday afternoon in the middle of July, to a town whose total population is about 4,000.

Every spring sees another surge of pilgrims to this baseball shrine, where admission is free.

Sometimes there are baseball games going on from first light to early night. Anybody can join in, just like at a family picnic. In late summer, many walk into the high stalks of corn surrounding the field, perhaps looking for their own baseball ghosts or family memories.

And even with the fans' disappointments over big-league baseball's squabbles, the simple *Field of Dreams* site remains immensely popular, unsullied by big-money madness.

"In fact, we've gotten lots of letters telling us that this is what baseball's all about," said Jacque Rahe, executive director of the Dyersville Chamber of Commerce. "They equate pure love of the game with our little field."

One of the best times to visit the field is on the second-to-last Sunday of each month, May through October, when "ghost ballplayers" wearing vintage uniforms emerge from surrounding cornfields, compete in a short exhibition game, and then play catch with some of the revelers.

Or come to the Field of Dreams Festival, in early September, which hosts a baseball charity game played by some of the legendary players in big-league history.

Just come.

FOR MORE INFORMATION

The field is located at 28963 Lansing Road in Dyersville, Iowa. A souvenir stand adjacent to the fields sells Field of Dreams memorabilia. Vials of dirt are available from a wooden box on the third base side of the diamond. The vials are free, but donations are accepted. The white farmhouse portrayed as the family's home in the movie stands off to the right of the field; it is not open to the public. For more Field of Dreams information, call (888) 875-8404; for Dyersville information, call (319) 875-2311.

10

Easter Awakenings

BLOOMINGTON

REGARDLESS OF RELIGIOUS AFFILIATION (IF ANY), MANY historians agree that the most potent figure in the history of the world is Jesus, who has been called "maker of one of the few revolutions which have lasted."

For nearly 2,000 years, millions of men and women for century after century have found his life and teachings overwhelmingly significant and moving. And while we'll let theologians and biblical scholars argue about the differences between the "historical Jesus" and the "Jesus Christ of faith," the fact that his message has influenced so many for so long establishes the man from Galilee as the preeminent personality in recorded times.

Now you can watch the most dramatic events of Jesus' life unfold in epic fashion during the American Passion Play in Bloomington, held annually from late March through early May, on Saturdays and Sundays only.

In its 73rd consecutive year, the four-hour-long Easter-season production passes across the stage of the Scottish Rites Temple auditorium and offers a unique perspective of Jesus' career.

"Unlike other Passion plays that simply tell the story of Easter Week, we start our dramatization by showing Jesus' entire three years of public ministry [preaching and healing] which leads to the story of the Passion," said Bill Barnard, play spokesperson. "Then we portray the final events in his life."

The production is strictly nondenominational, following events described in the King James version of the Bible.

It's set in first-century Galilee. More than 200 actors help re-create the desert outposts that Jesus called home; they range in age from 5 to 85—and some have been with the production for nearly 40 years.

There are 56 scene changes, taking theatergoers everywhere from the Sermon on the Mount and the miracle performed during the Wedding at Cana to Jesus' crucifixion, resurrection, and ascension—familiar "scenes" to any reader of history, parochial school veteran, or churchgoer.

Perhaps the most electrifying moment of the play comes during the scene that depicts Jesus calming a storm on the sea, then walking on the water, said Barnard. Lightning bolts, thunder, and rain (on the stage) add to the wonderment of the moment.

Nearly 15,000 people come to see the show during its run, some traveling from as far away as Pennsylvania to catch a glimpse of Easter-season hopefulness. And depending on your point of view, you might take a powerful message home, Barnard said.

In fact, you may discover that Jesus' message of faith, love, and justice is still our best hope for solving the problems of today.

For More Information

There is an admission charge for tickets; reservations are strongly recommended. The auditorium seats 1,300 people and is air-conditioned and wheelchair accessible. Bloomington is located about two-and-a-half hours southwest of Chicago. For information or reservations, call the production at (800) 354-9640; or contact the Bloomington-Normal Area Convention and Visitors Bureau, (800) 433-8226.

Spring

11

From Treasures to Trinkets

SANDWICH

WHETHER YOU'RE SEARCHING FOR TREASURES HIDDEN IN years-old strongboxes or trinkets that could be displayed on your antique breakfront, you can be pretty certain that what you purchase at the Sandwich Antiques Market will be the real McCoy.

That's because show manager Robert Lawler has his "antique police" on the prowl.

In fact, Lawler's standards are so strict that authentic collectibles sold at the 550-dealer market come with an unconditional 10-day money-back guarantee.

"There's no other place in Illinois where you can find such a deal," Lawler says.

Held about half a dozen times from spring through autumn at the Sandwich Fairgrounds on U.S. Route 34, the market is devoted to quality antiques and collectibles that are at least 20 years old, no longer in production, and had some intrinsic value when first made, Lawler says.

"No new merchandise, country crafts, or junk like T-shirts, tube socks, and hubcaps are allowed here," Lawler emphasized. "We carefully screen dealers and hold seminars to ensure a high caliber of antiques so the Sandwich experience is rewarding for everyone—both the buyer and dealer alike."

More than 300,000 items are offered at indoor buildings and outdoor booths on the 160-acre fairgrounds. Dealers come from more than 15 states. And there's something for everyone, whether you're willing to spend a whopping $13,000 on a Victorian wardrobe or just $75 for an oak chair.

However, Sandwich prides itself on fine 19th- and 20th-century American and English furniture, along with antique toys and all kinds of silver.

What's hot? The market is quite volatile, but American primitives and folk art have really caught collectors' fancies, Lawler says. In fact, you might be surprised that expensive "high-end" antiques (especially quality furniture) are selling briskly.

Here are some buying tips from experts for antique market rookies:

- If you are considering an expensive piece, bring a camera along, take a photo of the merchandise, and see how it might fit in with your home decor; also have it evaluated by another antiques dealer.

- A magnifying glass is a good tool to inspect hallmarks on silver and stamps on china, and to take close-up looks at jewelry.

- Another must is a magnet. It will help determine if your treasure is metal, brass-plated, or real brass.

- Prices are often flexible, but bargaining should be polite.

- Dealers often offer lower prices late in the day, since they do not want to carry everything back home.

With that in mind, it's time to turn all you treasure hunters loose.

For More Information

The Sandwich Antiques Market charges a small admission, with free parking. Furniture delivery can be arranged at the fairgrounds. Hours generally are 8:00 A.M. to 4:00 P.M., rain or shine. For more information on the market or directions, call the Sandwich Antiques Market, (773) 227-4464.

From Treasure to Trinkets

12

An Inn-Sider's Guide to Springtime Romance

ALL AROUND ILLINOIS

SOMETIMES THE MIDWEST'S SPRINGTIME MUD MONTHS CAN put a real damper on weekend fun. But you can make the weather work for you: If you can't go outside, why not spend a romantic weekend inn-side?

In fact, Illinois boasts several romantic inns that will make you forget about the weather and concentrate on that significant other. Before you know it, you'll be a coo-some two-some caught up in each other's delights—and even rain in Noah-like proportions won't distract you.

Here are a few of Illinois's best romantic getaways:

- Some of the most romantic vistas in Galena, a historic lead-mining town tucked into the northwest corner of Illinois, are claimed by the **Hellman Guest House**. Built on Quality Hill with views of Horsehose Mound and the town's several church steeples, gingerbread turrets, and surrounding bluffs, the inn is a romantic reminder of how glorious simple pleasures can still be as we approach the second millennium.

    The 1895 home has a magnificent interior, with cherry and oak woodwork, stained and leaded glass, and an opulent foyer that boasts its own fireplace. A huge parlor window reveals breathtaking views of Galena. So does the master bedroom, a guest bedchamber with a tower alcove that offers more incredible vistas. Or opt for the inn's luxury suite, complete with private fireplace and whirlpool. Call (815) 777-3638.

- For a quick romantic getaway just about an hour's drive west of Chicago, try the **Herrington**, located in historic Geneva. Nestled on the banks of the Fox River in a historic 1870s brick building, the inn offers guest rooms with riverside views, courtyard vistas, and whirlpool tubs. Call (630) 208-7433.

- **Pinehill Bed & Breakfast Inn** sits atop Jackson Hill in Oregon, a town located in the lush Rock River Valley. The inn's highest romantic quotient goes to its Somerset Maugham Room, named for the man of letters who often visited Pinehill in the 1930s. Today couples can enjoy the romance of a private wood-burning marble fireplace and a splashy whirlpool tub. Call (815) 732-2061.

- In the heart of Chicago's exclusive Gold Coast neighborhood, and just a short walk from the luxurious shopping of the Magnificent Mile, is the **Gold Coast Guest House**. This stately 1873 brick townhouse is a contemporary romantic retreat with classic designs spiced up by fine antiques. Guest bedchambers offer the best of both classic and contemporary decor, with second-floor rooms reached by climbing a winding spiral staircase; my favorite might be the one with a grand bay window overlooking the street. Dining takes place on a balcony overlooking the Great Room, opposite glass doors opening to a private garden. Call (312) 337-0361.

- Finally, another quick romantic getaway outside of Chicago brings you to the **Wheaton Inn**, which is opulent in the Colonial Williamsburg tradition even though the retreat was built in 1987. Several guest rooms boast private gas fireplaces, Jacuzzi tubs, towel warmers in bathrooms, and more pampering. Favorite bedchambers include the Woodward Room, with its Jacuzzi resting in front of a large bay window overlooking the inn's gardens; the McCormick Room, with its huge four-poster bed; and the Morton Room, which offers an alcoved ceiling, private fireplace, and four-and-one-half-feet-deep Jacuzzi, perfect for a romantic soak.

However, the most romantic of nights might be awaiting you and your honey in the Rice Room, where a Jacuzzi sits almost in the middle of the room, in front of a fireplace, while two skylights let you gaze at the stars outside.

The Wheaton Inn is located in the like-named western suburb; call (630) 690-2600.

An Insider's Guide to Springtime Romance

13

Lifestyles of the Rich and Famous

VERNON HILLS

YOU DON'T HAVE TO VISIT ITALY FOR UP-CLOSE PEEKS AT A Venetian palace, complete with old master paintings, priceless 17th-century tapestries, and its own outdoor stage (framed by 12-foot-tall Corinthian columns) that has hosted some of the greatest opera singers of all time.

In fact, all you have to do is head for the hills—Vernon Hills, to be exact. Because it's in that far north Chicago suburb where you can tour one of the most magnificent mansions ever built in the Midwest—it even has been compared to San Simeon, William Randolph Hearst's "castle" in central California.

The Cuneo Mansion and Gardens, an opulent Venetian-style estate, was built in 1914 as a private 32-room residence for Samuel Insull, founder of Commonwealth Edison.

However, the mansion gets its name from John Cuneo, Sr., who purchased the estate (which includes 75 acres of formal gardens, an outdoor stage, a swimming pool, and other upper-crust amenities) in 1937.

Cuneo's remarkable story of achievement is itself worth reviewing before describing this fabulous residence. Sent by his father to study economics at Yale and expected to take over his family's Chicago wholesale produce business,

Cuneo eventually dropped out of school. This angered his dad, who cut off all financial support to Cuneo.

Forced out into the marketplace on his own, Cuneo took a series of jobs in Chicago, eventually learning the printing business. He pleaded with his father for a small loan ($10,000) to purchase part ownership in a printing company. After many months of haggling, his father had a change of heart and gave the money to Cuneo.

More hard work led to remarkable success. Cuneo Press became the largest in the country, printing scores of the nation's top publications, including the *Saturday Evening Post*, *Life*, *Time*, and *Cosmopolitan*.

The mansion befits a man who achieved great wealth in his lifetime. Visitors begin tours in the Great Hall, a 40-foot-long room complete with Venetian archways, 10-foot columns, and a columned "balcony" that resembles similar structures along Venice's Grand Canal.

While the "hall" is graced with centuries-old tapestries, Oriental rugs, silver, and suits of armor, it is dominated by an intricately carved 1690 Italian trestle table—a gift from Cuneo's buddy William Randolph Hearst, who also liked to dabble in antiquities.

A peek into Cuneo's bedroom also reveals something about the nature of this complex man. His personal, mahogany four-poster bed is, itself, museum quality. But it doesn't speak nearly as powerfully as another piece of furniture sitting at the foot of his bed. That is the prie-dieu where the millionaire would nightly humble himself, saying bedtime prayers.

In fact, Cuneo was a profoundly dedicated Roman Catholic who gave generously to several Catholic charities. It's not surprising, then, that he would become a confidant to three popes. Cuneo, who religiously attended Mass, even had an ornate chapel built inside this mansion; this is where another good friend of his, Samuel Cardinal Stritch, often celebrated the Eucharist while archbishop of Chicago.

Spring

Cuneo's religion also influenced the Italian old master paintings he purchased for the house. One of the finest in his collection is "Madonna and Child with St. John the Baptist," by Andrea del Sarto, a 16th-century artist. It's said that Cuneo bought this piece at a 1957 New York auction for $125.

Of course, the Cuneo Mansion also flaunts an indoor swimming pool. But it's not just an ordinary pool; the millionaire modeled it after ancient (and elaborate) Roman baths.

You'll discover more wonderment while touring the estate grounds. Huge plots of formal gardens lend color and fragrance to the surroundings. Walk to the outdoor swimming pool, outlined by an elaborate white fence. Then proceed to the outdoor stage, flanked by those tall Corinthian columns.

Perhaps you'll even be inspired to break into your favorite aria.

For More Information

There's an admission fee for estate tours; you also can pay a lesser fee to view the grounds only. The estate is located at 1350 North Milwaukee Avenue, Vernon Hills, IL 60061; for more information, call (847) 362-3042.

Summer

14

Great Times at Great America

GURNEE

"FIVE . . . FOUR . . . THREE . . . TWO . . . ONE . . ."

BLAST OFF!!!

Where are we headed? Armstrong City—on the MOON! And to get there, all we have to do is hop aboard Space Shuttle America, the "only authentic, life-sized space shuttle replica in the Midwest."

Space Shuttle America is one of the super-attractions of Six Flags Great America in Gurnee, one of seven Six Flags theme parks that stretch across the country. They were the brainchild of Texas oilman Angus G. Wynne Jr., who after a visit to Disneyland in the 1950s decided to build a theme park that would be closer to home (Texas) with more emphasis on rides and family entertainment.

The 300-acre Gurnee park, opened in 1976, has six theme areas, each taking you into a different era of American history. They include Hometown Square (rural America in the 1920s), County Fair (a turn-of-the-century fun fest), Yukon Territory (the Klondike of the Gold Rush era), Yankee Harbor (a late 19th-century eastern seaboard fishing village), Orleans Place (the French Quarter of the 1850s), and Southwest Territory (featuring a Mexican plaza complete with cowboy shoot-'em-up stunt shows daily).

And while each area holds all kinds of thrills and chills for families, I'd rather showcase some of Great America's "shouldn't-miss" highlights:

- Standing five stories tall, **Space Shuttle America** readies to take you on your flight to the moon, with arrival at the United States' space colony of Armstrong City. Of course, the flight is routine—after all, people fly to and from the moon all the time.

  You enter the shuttle's hangar area, proceed through mission control, and then prepare for your flight. The space shuttle crew briefs you on in-flight procedures, buckles you into your seats, and begins the countdown. Feel the engines come to life beneath you. Listen to the roar at liftoff.

  However, the routine flight turns out to be anything but routine. Suddenly, the spacecraft encounters an uncharted asteroid field, whose orbiting rocks the size of Rhode Island could obliterate the shuttle. The crew must take evasive action, and before long, you're involved in a heart-pounding adventure of sheer survival.

  You even get to save Armstrong City from disaster.

  Actually, this 20-minute-long simulator ride, with its multisensory experiences, should thrill any Trekkie or "Deep Space Nine" fan. The park worked closely with NASA when building the simulator to give Great America guests the most authentic experience possible.

  It works!

- The **American Eagle** is a double-track wooden roller coaster that gives riders that old-time thrill of a jarring, wild ride. One of the world's greatest, it features a 147-foot drop on the first hill, guaranteed to generate loud screams and wails. That's because the angle of that first hill is 55 degrees, allowing coaster trains to attain speeds of almost 67 mph.

  I don't know why, but I'm fascinated by the inventory of materials that went into creating this fabulous ride. Imagine 1,060,000 board feet of lumber, 60,720 bolts, 30,600 pounds of nails, 9,000 gallons of white paint, and

2,000 concrete footings averaging 18 inches in diameter and 4.5 feet in depth. It also took more than 20,000 people-hours to build.

- **Iron Wolf** claims to be the "world's tallest and fastest stand-up looping roller coaster." It begins with a 90-foot drop on which it reaches speeds of nearly 55 mph—just as it enters a hair-raising 360-degree vertical loop. And that's only the beginning of your ride.

- **Shock Wave** is another heart-stopper. One of the world's tallest and fastest steel looping roller coasters, it climbs up to 180 feet before dive-bombing 155 feet; then it speeds up through seven loops at speeds exceeding 65 mph. Wow!

- **The Demon** is a spine-tingling roller coaster that plummets 82 feet, proceeds directly into two vertical loops, rockets through an illuminating display of light and sound effects, and finishes with two corkscrew loops.

- **Batman—The Ride** is the world's first suspended, outside looping coaster. What that means is that there's no seat; you're suspended in almost thin air by a contraption that grabs you, keeping you firmly and safely in place. Your feet dangle. Your stomach turns. It's a scream.

- **Looney Tunes National Park** and **Camp Cartoon Network** are the new cornerstones of the Yukon Territory. They feature more than four acres of new rides and attractions for smaller kids, with all your favorite Bugs Bunny characters.

    For example, Yosemite Sam Tour takes visitors for a ride on the Looney Tooter Train or a climb up Pepe Le Pew's Peak. At Camp Cartoon Network, you can ride in the

Great Times at Great America

Scooby-Doo Mystery Machine, take a cruise in the Flint-mobile, or experience roller-coaster thrills on Spacely's Sprocket Rockets.

Of course, there are plenty of other attractions that the entire family can enjoy. **Sky Trek Tower** carries guests 285 feet into the wild blue yonder until reaching a cabin that rotates 360 degrees for panoramic views of the park and surrounding landscape. **Roaring Rapids** may sound scary, but it's a family favorite, especially on hot, sunny days; that's because the white-water rapids expedition is guaranteed to leave you soaked.

Let's not forget **Bugs Bunny Land**, a wonderland fantasy for little kids featuring more than two dozen fun rides; also catch the "Toonite Show," yet another talk show, this one hosted by that "quazy wabbit" himself And the **Imax** *Blue Planet* film features footage shot by astronauts during five space shuttle missions on a seven-story screen; this includes never-before-seen views of planet Earth—including space vistas of the swirling ferocity of Hurricane Hugo, electrical storms at night, volcanic eruptions, and more.

Finally, note that Six Flags Great America produces several special events throughout the year. These may include anything from Joyfest, a Christian music summer celebration, to Fright Fest, an annual Halloween scarum.

FOR MORE INFORMATION

Six Flags Great America's regular season is spring weekends (mid-April to mid-May), then daily through Labor Day weekend, and fall weekends through the end of September. For admission prices, hours, and other information, contact Six Flags Great America, P.O. Box 1776, Gurnee, IL 60031; (847) 249-1776.

Summer

15

Riding the Rails to Weekend Adventure

Far North, West, and South Suburban Chicago

TRAFFIC WAS BUMPER-TO-BUMPER ON THE DAN RYAN. AFTER a five-minute wait in steaming July heat, cars begin to move. I drove about six feet before stopping dead. Again. And again. And again . . .

My family and I had been on the road 90 minutes, trying to make our way from Chicago's Near Northwest Side toward Kankakee and points south for a getaway weekend. Expressway signs shouted that we had only reached 67th Street. We sat. And waited.

It was quiet inside the car. Too quiet. Suddenly, while "Peter Pan" played for the third consecutive time on the tape deck, all hell broke loose.

"My seat belt's too tight! I want to get out of here!" screamed daughter Kate, then four years old. Dayne, her two-year-old sister, wailed, "I want to go back to my own home!" Uncontrollable weeping follows. It's a dramatic kiddie coup de grace, very effective on parents whose nerves are already as prickly as porcupine quills.

That's my most vivid memory of one summer's "car trip to hell." But with endless road construction blocking, botching, and stalling Chicago-area traffic in almost every direction, even more cases of "auto-erratic dementia" are certain to strike weekend wanderers.

There is a cure—hop on the rails. Metra's commuter trains offer one of the best deals around. The 495-mile Metropolitan Rail system, serving about 230 stations in Cook, DuPage, Lake, Will, McHenry, and Kane Counties, sells a ticket good for unlimited riding on Saturdays and Sundays. These trains can whisk weekenders in air-conditioned comfort to the "front door" of riverside villages, suburban museums, art galleries, quaint towns, historic attractions, and special events.

So forget the traffic. Smirk smugly at road warriors sweltering in godless gridlock. You can play it cool on the train. Here's a sampling of the best traffic-beating summer weekend rail getaways.

Best Bang for the Bucks

Want to enjoy lakeside resort pleasures and pristine wilderness at Illinois's only on-the-beach hotel without ever touching the steering wheel of your car? Head to Illinois Beach State Park and Resort in Zion, which hugs the waters of Lake Michigan just before it's sliced and diced by the Wisconsin state line.

The Metra C&NW-North train gets you hassle-free from Chicago to Zion; a lodge courtesy car picks you up and delivers you to heaven. There's six miles of sand beaches and shoreline perfect for sunbathing, walking barefoot in the water, making sand castles, or taking a dip. Hiking and biking trails abound through the heavily wooded state park landscape, where you're likely to spot wandering deer, foxes, and other furry pals.

The handsome lodge features large rooms and a surprisingly good full-service restaurant. Kids will splash for hours in the 80-foot-long lakeside indoor swimming pool. Adults can sweat off indulgences in a state-of-the-art health club. Room rates range from less than $80 on up—and kids are free! Make weekend reservations as soon as possible, be sure to tell the lodge you're coming on Metra, and give the exact arrival time so a car can be waiting for you at the train station. For more information, call the lodge at (847) 625-7300 or the park at (847) 662-4828.

Fish (Rail) Tales

From the hubbub of people power at downtown Chicago's Union Station to no-worry "deep-sea" coho fishing thrills in no time at all—that's the story when you take Metra's C&NW-North line to Waukegan, the self-proclaimed "Capital of the Coho Coast." This 12-mile stretch of northern Lake Michigan harbors some of the salmon family's most legendary lunkers.

Just walk one block east on Madison Street from the train station to reach the charter captains' pier, where you can choose from nearly 30 vessels waiting to provide on-the-sea adventures. For about $50 or so per person (three-person minimum), you get a half-day's worth of angling for coho or steelhead, led by a professional fish-buster. In June, the city's annual Coho Salmon Derby offers prizes for the biggest daily, weekly, and fest-long catches. Charter boat captains report that steelhead can run up to a whopping 24 pounds.

Other Waukegan delights include a historic district walking tour (maps available), kid fun at Siever Park, and North Avenue's boutiques, art galleries, and restaurants. For fishing information, call (847) BIG-FISH; for Waukegan information, call the Lake County Chamber of Commerce, (847) 249-3800.

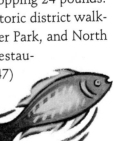

Riding the Rails to Weekend Adventure

Metra Mini-Tours

Geneva   Geneva's only 35 miles west of Chicago, but it's like another world. Founded in 1833 as a trading center on the banks of the Fox River, the town is proud of its National Landmark District, which includes more than 200 architecturally important buildings; its ornamental Victorian homes on gaslit, tree-lined streets; a museum full of history; a summer repertory theater; and more than a hundred distinctive antique and specialty shops.

State, Third, and Campbell Streets are jammed with boutiques and restaurants. Especially noteworthy is the Mill Race Inn, nestled on the edge of the Fox River, serving up classic dining fare and river views. Geneva on the Dam (River Lane), a refurbished limestone iron company building, offers boutiques, riverside walking paths, and alfresco dining. And right on the river's shoreline is The Herrington, a luxurious bed-and-breakfast whose rooms are equipped with everything from waterside balconies and fireplaces to romantic whirlpools.

Kids will love to roam at Island Park, where they can feed ducks or create their own fun. Visit during June's annual Swedish Days for parades, crafts, carnival rides, and live entertainment. The Metra C&NW train station puts you within walking distance of all the action. For Geneva information, call (630) 232-6060.

St. Charles   Ride a double-decked riverboat, boogie at a festival celebrating the Fox River, and enjoy performances of internationally known musicians in historic St. Charles. The town, huddled on wooded hills stretching down to the Fox River, is dappled with turn-of-the-century architecture and whimsical boutiques.

You can explore lots of shops and side streets in this 150-year-old village, cruise the Fox on double-decked paddle-wheelers, sip soda fountain treats, and even discover antique treasures.

History comes alive at the Dunham Hunt Museum, whose namesake was a local 19th-century breeder of Percheron horses. The Market, a restored lumber mill, houses some 25 stores offering such items as American primitives, hand-wrought jewelry, and Old English handicrafts. Rent a bike and glide along the Fox River Trail, or sample the Great Western Trail, which winds through open prairie.

Summer highlights include Pride of the Fox River Festival, in June, with funny-raft races, food, and live entertainment like The Gatlins and Three Dog Night; and the St. Charles Art and Music Festival in July, a major cultural event featuring international piano contests with world-class musicians, jazz masters, classical concertos, pop renditions, and more.

Take the Metra train to the Geneva stop, pick up a Pace bus, get off at Main Street in St. Charles, about a 10-minute ride. Really hearty visitors walk the bike trail from the train station to St. Charles, a two-mile trek. Or catch a cab, which meets all incoming trains. For St. Charles information, call (800) 777-4373.

Naperville Naperville's Riverwalk is a dream weaver's delight. The linear park along the DuPage River offers romantic covered bridges, bubbling water fountains, and red brick pathways winding through landscaped greenery. Peek at paintings in the Riverwalk Art Gallery, enjoy a summertime concert at the amphitheater, or rent a paddleboat just down the path in renovated Riverwalk Quarries.

Chicago Avenue and Washington Street are where you'll find boutiques, art galleries, and eateries. 5th Avenue Station, a restored furniture factory, offers specialty shops, restaurants, and a Farmers' Market (Saturdays, May through October).

Don't miss Naper Settlement, a living-history reconstruction of a 19th-century Illinois prairie village located in the southwestern downtown area. The 12-acre "town" is inhabited by costumed interpreters who guide you through 24 historic residences and businesses spanning from 1830 to the turn of the century. Visit on Militia Sunday (in June) or Turn-of-the-Century Days (July) for more frontier-style fun and music. Call (630) 420-6010.

Or take the kids to Centennial Beach, billed as the "world's third largest body of chlorinated water." If you get a motel room, rent a car and make a weekend of it. Other nearby attractions include Fermilab and Argonne Laboratory's prairie buffalo herd; the 1,500-acre Morton Arboretum; Cantigny, the historic 500-acre estate of Col. Robert McCormick that boasts gardens and a World War II museum; Blackberry Historical Farm Village, an 1840 pioneer farm, complete with pony rides and a petting barn on 60 acres; and the Old Graue Mill and Museum, a working waterwheel gristmill.

From Metra's Burlington Northern Line stop in Naperville, it's just a four-block walk (go south) along Washington Street to the heart of downtown. For Naperville information, call (630) 355-4141.

Betting on Fun

This Fox River Valley city is betting the ranch on riverboat casinos. In fact, Aurora, a town of nearly 100,000 on the south end of the broad, tranquil valley, is home to two 600-passenger floating gambling dens. Called the *City of Lights I* and *II*, these unlimited-wagering casinos offer everything from blackjack and poker to slot machines and craps. Call (800) 888-7777.

If betting isn't your thing, you can enjoy yourself at Aurora's newly refurbished Paramount Arts Centre. This restored vintage 1931 theater, sitting on Stolp Island, presents all kinds of star-studded entertainment, from Tom Jones to Liza Minnelli and Howie Mandel. For a schedule of concerts and shows, call (630) 896-7676.

And the city's downtown area also invites you to examine its interesting architecture—including many buildings with ornate terra-cotta trim.

South Shore Excursion Trains

From its passenger hub at Randolph and Michigan, the Chicago South Shore Railroad can whisk traffic-avoiding travelers to dune-filled beaches and outlet mall paradises. And while these attractions are technically located in Indiana, their just-across-the-state-line status has transformed them into virtual Chicago suburbs.

Chesterton Get off at Dunes Park in Chesterton, Indiana, and it's just a short walk to mountains of windblown sand, expansive flat beaches, and quiet nature trails in Indiana Dunes State Park and National Lakeshore. Kids love to scale Mt. Baldy; it's a legwearying climb of 135 feet to reach the summit. But the reward is panoramic views of Lake Michigan and the hazy skyline of Chicago.

Of course, rolling down the sandy slope is even more fun than the climb. And the National Park Service offers ranger-led programs and activities throughout the year. Weekend family and special rail excursion fares are available. For national lakeshore information, call (219) 926-7561.

Michigan City It's just a seven-block walk from Michigan City's 11th Street train station to Lighthouse Place, a massive outlet mall that features designer names and great bargains. (To get there, go two blocks west on 11th Street, then five blocks north on Wabash.) Especially tempting is the Ralph Lauren outlet store.

Also nearby is The Works, an indoor mall, and several historic homes surrounding the shopping district have been transformed into specialty boutiques.

Hearty trekkers can reach the Lake Michigan waterfront, where they can enjoy pier walks out to a historic lighthouse, Washington Park's sandy beaches, and a charming zoo that's a real kid pleaser. Travelers also can hire taxis, which gather at a 24-hour cab stand right next to the South Shore train station, for the Michigan City whirls. For Michigan City information, call (219) 874-6221.

For either above-mentioned excursion, you should treat yourself royally and overnight at the Creekwood Inn, located just off I-94 at U.S. Routes 20/35. This 13-room gem, constructed in English Cottage design, is nestled on 33 tree-covered acres of walnut, oak, and pine near a fork in tiny Walnut Creek. Massive hand-hewn wooden ceiling beams, a parlor with a huge brick fireplace, and classic guest rooms (some with their own fireplaces and terraces) make this a wonderful retreat. In fact, maybe you'd rather get off the train at Michigan City, take a cab to the inn, and spend your entire weekend right there. For reservations, call (219) 872-8357.

FOR MORE INFORMATION

For more rail, travel, and touring information, call the Chicago Office of Tourism, Chicago Cultural Center, (312) 744-2400; the Illinois Bureau of Tourism, (800) 223-0121; or Metra (commuter trains), (312) 322-6777.

72

Summer

16

State Fair Time

SPRINGFIELD

ABOUT NOW IS WHEN THE FANTASIES FLASH.

I see state police patrolling the grounds on rollerblades, wearing shorts, safari shirts, and pith helmets. A life-size cow sculpted entirely of pure butter. Racing pigs dressed in colorful jockey silks.

Am I going completely wacko? Nope, it's just Illinois State Fair time again.

Here's where country meets kitsch, where animals are prissied up fancier than a Vidal Sassoon makeover, where you can buy anything from "miracle" frying pans to a vibrating sofa, where you're just as likely to see the Hee Haw Honeys as Smashmouth.

Almost a million people party with the animals at this annual mid-August livestock, horticulture, home economics, and other "best of" bash. Not surprising, since it has been long renowned as one of the country's premier agricultural showcases.

The fair always kicks off with the Twilight Parade, winding through the state capital's streets to the fairgrounds; the procession is usually led by the current governor (or should I say, in this case, strolling chief executive?).

The fair also dispenses some of the most kitschy down-home fun around:

- A largest boar contest is a real battle of the bulge. Held in the Open Swine Building, thousand-pound tusked porkers strut their potbellied stuff in hopes of the heavyweight porker title.

- Take the Dinotour for a walk through the prehistoric rain forest, filled with mechanical dinosaurs, spooky fog, and creepy plants. Don't worry—*Jurassic Park* was just a movie, right?

- An unforgettable sight is the life-size sculpted butter cow, a creamy creation of Norma Lyon, who has fashioned this moo-tiful eatwork for 25 butterful years. It's on view daily at the Dairy Building.

- You can bet your bass that fish will be bitin' at the Hawg Trough, a 5,000-gallon aquarium in Outdoor World. Expert bassmasters will demonstrate how to hook award-winning bass. But it seems pretty easy when they're just swimming around a giant fishbowl.

- "Here, Porky!" shouts a woman onstage. But is she calling her husband or her prize porker? Find out during the whoops and hollers of the Husband/Hog Calling Contest, slated in the Swine Barn. The louder the vocal belt, the bigger the prize.

- For an udderly good time, attend the Moo Moo Classic at the Livestock Center. Four-person relay tag teams race to squeeze the most milk into their buckets in pursuit of the prestigious State Fair Milking Title. Of course, you can try your hand at milking a cow for a quarter at the Cow Barn.

- Counting Crows isn't just a rock band. It's a 30-minute contest in the Orr Building. Winning roosters (those who crow the most times, after responding to spoken words, shouts, handclapping, and other incentives from their owners) for the first four days participate in a grand champion crow-off.

- Daredevils looking for thrills and chills will want to try the Rip Line. For about $15, you stand atop a 50-foot tower, grab a handle, and slide down a thin steel cable while dangling feet-first in the air.

For more "normal" fun, head to Conservation World, offering free voyageur canoe rides, birds of prey show-and-tells, wild turkey trapping demonstrations, and even Smokey the Bear. However, its headliner act remains Scheer's Lumberjack Show, whose Hayward, Wisconsin, woodsmen compete in log rolling, ax throwing, and pole climbing.

Happy Hollow, site of the fair's midway and carnival rides, sometimes also features "Circo de Espectacular," with its daredevil circus acts and a "wheel walker" who boldly climbs to the top of a 104-foot Ferris wheel—while it's moving! Circus shows are slated daily.

And one of the biggest crowd pleasers is live entertainment offered daily at the Main Grandstand. Big-name national acts offer something for everyone; past headliners have been rappers Salt-N-Pepa, middle-of-the-road crooner Barry Manilow, deejay Wolfman Jack's '50s rock 'n' roll show, country music powerhouse Vince Gill, alternative rock Meat Puppets and Jawbox, perennial favorites The Beach Boys, even the highbrow Symphonic Pops Orchestra

State Fair Time

of Chicago. Tickets generally range from $10 to $15; call the box office at (217) 782-1979, or any Ticketmaster location.

FOR MORE INFORMATION

Admission is charged for the Illinois State Fair (children 12 and under are free). There is a parking fee. For hours and other information, contact the Illinois State Fair, (217) 782-6661.

Summer

17

Home of the Man of Steel

METROPOLIS

FORGET THE MIGHTY MORPHIN POWER RANGERS. OR THAT pointy-headed weenie named Batman. Even Arnold Schwarzenegger is a wimpy geek compared to the Man of Steel.

Superman—strange visitor from another planet, more powerful than a locomotive, able to leap tall buildings in a single bound—continues the fight for Truth, Justice, and the American Way. Don't believe me? Find out for yourself during the Superman Celebration, an annual June festival headquartered in his "hometown" of Metropolis.

Every year, Superman returns to this little city located at the southern tip of Illinois near the Kentucky border to visit old friends and watch family-style fun and games like the Superman tug-of-war, Little Miss Supergirl and Mr. Superboy pageants, Super Dog Contest, and the Super Trek Bike Ride. (The superfun also usually includes a traveling Superman museum collection and film festival.)

But the big attraction is the Man of Steel himself. You can see him in action in the town's Superman drama, a suspenseful live outdoor show that, in past performances, has incorporated helicopter stunts, machine gun-toting bad guys, bumbling cub reporter Jimmy Olsen, ace scribe Lois Lane, and . . . Great Caesar's ghost, *Daily Planet* editor Perry White.

Of course, Superman rescues everybody.

A stroll through town reveals just how crazy Metropolis

is about its favorite son. Such Superman paraphernalia as collector stamps, 3-D portraits, comic and coloring books, buttons, and official hometown T-shirts is everywhere.

Want to chat with the Super One himself? You'll find him browsing among antique car displays, flea market booths, bike-riding contestants, and road race runners throughout the weekend.

You can even step into a phone booth (located at the Massac County Chamber of Commerce, 608 Market Street) to experience the embarrassment Superman must feel when climbing out of his mild-mannered reporter suit into his yellow, red, and blue superhero tights and talk to the Man of Steel direct on the telephone.

Is Metropolis actually the home of Superman? Well, in 1972 the town proclaimed itself to be the real thing. In fact, city officials claim it's the only town named Metropolis in the United States—so what more proof do you need? It even has a newspaper called the *Metropolis Planet*, although it's not a daily and no one named Clark Kent currently works there.

Besides an opportunity to have a photo taken with Superman at the festival, you can opt for a snapshot session next to a 35-foot-long Superman billboard along the highway leading into town. Better yet, pose alongside the massive eight-foot-tall Man of Steel statue on Market Street.

Only one thing bothers me about Metropolis's claim to fame. If this Illinois town, situated farther south than Richmond, Virginia, really is the home of Superman, how come he doesn't talk with a Dixie twang, y'all?

For More Information

Most superactivities take place at the Riverfront. Metropolis is about six hours south of Chicago. For information about the festival or other Superman attractions, contact Massac County Convention and Visitors Bureau, (618) 524-2714.

18

Prairie Primer

MORRIS

IMAGINE A PLACE WHERE PRAIRIE GRASSES AS HIGH AS A horse's shoulder roll in the gentle breeze like an ocean swell. Where wildflowers such as fall asters, black-eyed susans, and goldenrod are scattered across the flatlands like a colorful carpet. A place where deer and coyote still roam virgin prairie soils.

You can find that place at Goose Lake Prairie State Natural Area, a precious gem of about 2,500 acres of virgin Illinois prairie that has been spared from the sodbuster's plow and looks much as it did more than 150 years ago when pioneers first settled the Midwest.

Yet this prairie paradise is only 60 miles southwest of Chicago.

Goose Lake Prairie is one of the largest preserves in the tallgrass region of North America. Historically, Illinois once was virtually covered by prairieland—rich black soil, thick and abundant in organic matter, that when cultivated yielded fabulous crop production. The virgin prairie environment supported tallgrass and wildflowers and only a few scattered trees and shrubs.

As settlement took place, the prairies were converted to farmland, which drastically changed the look of the frontier that had confronted early pioneers.

Today, Goose Lake Prairie is a reminder of the virgin prairie that was home to Potawatomi Indians, Canadian trappers, and early settlers of the "Old Northwest."

There are a number of ways to enjoy this peaceful journey into the past. The Tallgrass Nature Trail winds 1.5 miles through the prairie grasses, marshes, and glacial potholes that cover the landscape. Trail-guide pamphlets (whose numbered text passages correspond to numbered posts along the way) describe this unique grassland environment that seemingly engulfs visitors.

Look closely at the prairie grasses surrounding you—big bluestem is the trademark and dominant grass of this soil. Its dense roots enable it to flourish, and it's an excellent forage crop, used by settlers to feed livestock. Wildflowers commonly grow among the grass; you'll see woolly sunflower in the fall, and white and cream indigo, rattlesnake-master, and prairie rose in the spring and summer.

Other grasses include switchgrass, little bluestem, Indian grass, and cordgrass; you can spot these along the trail and near the banks of drainage ditches. Under ideal conditions, switchgrass can reach a height of seven feet. Indian grass will grow almost a foot higher!

At one point along the trail, you can look east and see the Dresden Bluffs—they mark the confluence of the Kankakee and Des Plaines Rivers. You'll also spot some of the structures of the Dresden Nuclear Power Plant off in the distance. Note that these are more than 2.5 miles away; it gives you an idea of how the prairie could dwarf distances and fool settlers into thinking their journeys would be shorter than they actually were—sometimes causing great hardship.

Also notice the prairie potholes, left by the retreat of the great glaciers of the last Ice Age more than 10,000 years ago. It riddled Goose Lake with these shallow depressions; however, they soon filled with water and became havens for wildlife.

Today, these potholes draw tens of thousands of migrating wild ducks and Canada geese in spring and fall, putting on a spectacular skyshow for visitors. The rare Henslow's sparrow also can be found here, along with the plains pocket gopher and other animals.

Perhaps the most popular feature at Goose Lake is its floating bridge, which stretches 380 feet across a marsh. Walking on the squishy contraption always causes squeals of delight among kids.

It's this very "water on the prairie" or seasonally marshy landscape that contributed to the survival of Goose Lake Prairie in its natural state. The land, generally too wet to support crops and too expensive to drain (in pioneer times), was home to buffaloes, wolves, prairie chickens, and otters. Early groups of Indian mound builders resided near this site; in fact, 19 mounds were uncovered northwest of the park and more have been found south of the Illinois River.

Tribes of the Illini Confederation settled and farmed the area, with the most famous inhabitant being the Potawatomi chief Shabbona, who came to the aid of white settlers during the 1832 Black Hawk War. Eventually, his tribe was forced onto a reservation in Kansas in 1836, but the chief defied the move, returned to his native lands, and is buried in the Evergreen Cemetery of Morris.

While a Canadian trapper regularly hunted Goose Lake in the 1820s, William Hoge was the first permanent white settler in Grundy County. Another early resident described the area as "almost treeless," but livestock grazing and the lack of prairie fires every few years allowed hawthorn trees to invade and flourish.

Another interesting piece of Goose Lake Prairie history is the vanished hamlet of Jug Town, a settlement that began in 1853 and grew to more than 50 families who made drain tiles, water jugs, and pottery from clay mined on the edge of Goose Prairie. The town had "pottery factories," homes, two boardinghouses, a school, a blacksmith shop, a general store, kilns—and a saloon.

prairie primer

Most townies were New Yorkers and immigrants from England and Ireland. Then, suddenly, the community "gave out." We still aren't quite sure why it was deserted. All that remains of Jug Town is an old drying shed, kilns, and part of the school building.

At the park's interpretative center, free auto tour maps lead you on a journey that highlights some of the park's history, geology, and ecology. Exhibits explain the prairie history and ecology. And a number of year-round naturalist-led programs are offered; check with park rangers for current schedules.

When the snow starts flying, a cross-country ski clinic provides ski instruction and other schussing and equipment tips. Then get out and hit the trails: Goose Lake Prairie has almost seven miles of beginners' cross-country ski trails and another six miles for advanced schussers. Maps, a warming house, and hot drinks are available.

What about THE Goose Lake? Well, that namesake body of water no longer exists; it was drained before the turn of the century to mine the valuable clay below the lake bottom. Records show that the lake spread over nearly 1,000 acres, its water "so covered with ducks and geese the water wasn't visible."

What remains is a series of ponds, prairie potholes, and marshes—and a fascinating glimpse of Illinois more than 150 years ago.

For More Information

Guided hikes and family educational programs take place on many weekends throughout the year. For more information and a schedule of naturalist-led and special events, contact Goose Lake Prairie State Natural Area, Site Superintendent, 5010 North Jugtown Road, Morris, IL 60450; (815) 942-2899.

Summer

19

Bearing Up Under the Sun

PLATTEVILLE, WISCONSIN

DURING A TYPICAL JULY, THE CUBS ALREADY HAVE SUNK TO the bottom of the National League, the White Sox's only excitement is the "Big Hurt," and all-world Chicago Bulls' basketball star Michael Jordan is retired again.

For Illinois summer sports fans, there's only one thing left: cheesehead football.

Yep, under the broiling sun of Platteville, Wisconsin, about 30 minutes north of Galena and just across the Illinois-Wisconsin border, the Chicago Bears toil in an outdoor oven otherwise known as their summer training camp. And their two-a-day workouts annually draw huge crowds of spectators from Chicago and other Bear dens in the state.

Up-close peeks at the action, audible grunts and groans, and the chance to see if the Bears' much-disdained owner Michael McCaskey will show up again in a ridiculous panama hat are among the perks for fans willing to boil along the sun-baked sidelines of the University of Wisconsin-Platteville practice fields on Southwest Road. Admission is free.

"Lots of times, it's just a matter of reaching across practice-field ropes to grab an autograph or ask for a photograph with your favorite player," said a spokesperson for Platteville's Chamber of Commerce. "You can't do that at Soldier Field in Chicago," where the Bears play all their regular-season home games.

The sweltering heat usually begins in mid-July, just as the team goes onto the practice field for two-hour, twice-daily workouts. A head-banging scrimmage, held in Pioneer Stadium just a few days after training camp opens, is another delight. Reserved and general admission seats are available.

Platteville's business community joins in the Bears mania. Stores continue the practice of "adopting" a Bears player, then decorating their windows with pictures of their chosen warrior. Local watering holes also are sometimes frequented by certain players; it's another good place to meet them socially.

Remember that the Bears are part of what's been called the "Cheesehead League"; they're one of four National Football League teams holding summer training camp in Wisconsin. To see these behemoths in action, contact the Kansas City Chiefs in River Falls, (715) 425-2533; the New Orleans Saints in LaCrosse, (800) 658-9424; and the Green Bay Packers in Green Bay, (800) 236-3976.

Also note that since Platteville is just over the Illinois border in Wisconsin, many Bears fans overnight in motels, hotels, and bed-and-breakfasts in Galena, Illinois. Then they can watch football by day and still have the late afternoon and evening for exploring this lead-mining boomtown with its turn-of-the-century architecture, scores of boutiques, art galleries, craft stores, antique shops, and fine restaurants. And nearby Dubuque, Iowa, offers more chancy fun—a cruise on a riverboat casino, which offers unlimited-stakes wagering.

For More Information

For more Chicago Bears summer training camp information, contact the Platteville Chamber of Commerce, (608) 348-8888. Galena's toll-free number is (800) 747-9377.

20

Scottish Fling

OAK BROOK

IMAGINE WATCHING BURLY MEN WEARING KILTS FLIP telephone poles end over end. Or use rings and chains to toss around 56-pound stones. Maybe you'd rather see these studlies grab a three-pronged pitchfork to sail hay-filled burlap bags over high horizontal poles.

How about witnessing barefoot "chest-to-chest" wrestling where matches are lost by the first competitor who touches the ground with any part of his body other than his feet?

Weirdoes? Australian-rules football gone even wackier? Nope, these ancient "heavy" athletic events are all part of the annual Illinois St. Andrew Scottish Highland Games, usually held every Father's Day weekend in Oak Brook.

Bagpipes are calling you to the 100-acre campus of the Chicago College of Osteopathic Medicine, perhaps an appropriate site for these traditional tests of brawn used by Scottish clans to determine the Cro-Magnon Schwarzenegger of the kilt-clad bunch. It always promises to be one of the best ceilidhs (pronounced "kay-lees") around.

The old-fashioned all-day Scottish hoedown also delights with scores of ethnic entertainers, including lilting folk singers, Highland fling dancers prancing to marches and jigs, and knock-your-socks-off bagpipers playing Ceol Beig (little music) while coaxing haunting wails and squealing reels out of their instruments.

Action officially begins during a Scottish Country Dance Ball. Costumed dancers swirl and glide to live ethnic music, demonstrating highly choreographed, intricate styles of traditional Scottish hoofing. It's quite a spectacle, especially when you note that this graceful dance form is considered the forerunner of American square dancing. Admission for spectators is free, along with samples of Walkers Scottish Shortbread.

At the fest itself, you'll see a blaze of kilts at the colorful Parade of Tartans; pipe band competitions begin soon afterward and continue throughout the day; Highland dancers and Sword Dance competitions also take place; and the Massing of the Bands closing ceremony, a kaleidoscope of tartans and squealing bagpipes, is usually slated for early evening.

Also enjoy live entertainment throughout the day as Celtic instrumentalists, singers, and dancers wrap the fest in an audio quilt of Scottish tunes. Everybody must learn some country-dance steps just to show they've had a good time.

Kids can watch champion dogs herd sheep; sample Scottish meat pie, black pudding, and bridies; learn about targes and dirks; listen to magical storytellers; or play a round of mini-golf at a scaled-down St. Andrews.

Of course, everyone's favorite attraction remains the Scottish "heavy events." Cheer as athletes test their strength and skills in games like the hammer throw (toss 16- and 22-pound, 4-foot-long hammers for distance); weight throws (28- and 56-pound weights); clachnert (distance pitch of a 16-pound stone sphere); sheaf tosses (pitchfork throwing of burlap bags filled with hay); and Highland wrestling.

Don't miss the Caber Toss, where behemoths attempt to lift 120-pound, 20-foot-long telephone poles and flip them end over end.

Junior athletic contests are scaled-down versions of the strong-man events; here the caber measures only six feet long. Other competitions are Donald Dinnie wrestling (similar to American collegiate wrestling), stone puts (distance throws), and the javelin toss.

Perhaps the most interesting junior contest features the atlatl, a weapon and hunting tool used by prehistoric man. The atlatl is a peculiar-looking spear with a hooked stick attached to it, adding length to the thrower's arm and momentum to his toss. It's heaved for distance.

And before the heavy-events competitions, you can watch some of the nation's top Scottish-games athletes demonstrate these foreign skills.

FOR MORE INFORMATION

Admission is charged (kids under six free); price includes parking, air-conditioned shuttle bus to and from parking area, and a $1 tax-deductible contribution to the Scottish Home, a retirement and nursing facility in North Riverside.

For more festival information, contact the DuPage County Convention and Visitors Bureau, (800) 232-0502.

21

Land of the Mound Builders

COLLINSVILLE

IT'S RARE THAT A MIDWEST ARCHAEOLOGICAL SITE CAN BE
mentioned in the same breath as the Pyramids, the Taj
Mahal, the Great Wall of China, and the monumental structures of Rome.

But southwestern Illinois claims bragging rights to one
significant archaeological find: Cahokia Mounds, the largest
prehistoric Indian city north of Mexico.

And it's not until you climb the stairs to the top of Monks
Mound, a 100-foot-tall, four-tiered platform built between
A.D. 900 and A.D. 1200, and gaze out over the acres of
Cahokia Mounds State Historic and World Heritage Site that
you realize the ancients who lived here had to be techno-
logical wizards of the first order.

Located on a fertile floodplain just six miles east of the
Mississippi River, Cahokia (called the ancient "City of the
Sun") was crammed with 20,000 residents by A.D. 1100.

This means that more people lived here 10,000 years ago,
long before history was recorded, than live in Collinsville
today.

Cahokia's pole-walled homes with grass-thatched roofs
were arranged in rows around open plazas. More than 100
man-made earthen mounds dotted the city, and a wooden
wall about 15 feet high surrounded 300 sacred acres of the
central city.

Today 65 mounds remain, along with an advanced scientific wooden sun calendar and hundreds of artifacts housed in an $8.2 million interpretive center, combining to tell the story of a sophisticated culture whose prehistoric city acted as a mecca for other ancient Midwest settlements.

First-time visitors should head directly to the interpretive center for a 15-minute audiovisual presentation explaining ancient urban life at Cahokia. You'll learn that while the agrarian Woodland Indians lived here for about 200 years beginning in A.D. 700, a more sophisticated second culture, the Mississipian Indians, emerged about A.D. 850.

This advanced culture brought highly developed technologies of science and engineering, developed urban living on the floodplain, and improved agriculture.

How did they do it?

Scientists aren't quite sure. For example, these ancient people had to move more than 22 million cubic feet of earth just to build Monks Mound. It was made entirely from dirt dug with tools of stone, wood, or shell, then transported on people's backs in baskets to the mound sites.

Built in stages stretching over 300 years, Monks Mound is the largest prehistoric earthen construction in the New World. Its base covers 14 acres, and a massive building (more than 100 feet long, 48 feet wide, and 50 feet high) stood on top, home to the city's ruler, who could look out on his people below.

Other mounds, built in platform, ridge-top, and conical formations (several of which you can visit during outdoor walking tours on marked trails), were used as temples, homes for the nobility, and burial.

Archaeologists also have uncovered four or five "sun calendars," which are functionally similar to England's Stonehenge. Constructed about A.D. 1000, the remains of Cahokia's "Woodhenge" (which resembles a circle of tall timbers) is really a sophisticated scientific tool for determining the seasons and scheduling ceremonial activities.

Viewed from the center of the circle, sunrises align with perimeter posts marking the "date" of the year.

Inside the interpretive center, a visitor favorite is the Exhibit Gallery, where you can walk through a panoramic re-creation of one of Cahokia's ancient city neighborhoods. Simulations of Cahokia archaeological excavations are displayed. And an extensive collection of unearthed artifacts used in both daily chores and ceremonial functions include an impressive number that have sun symbols inscribed on them—a possible indication that these Indians worshipped the sun as a deity or spirit.

While a visit to Cahokia Mounds provides an unforgettable weekend ramble any time of the year, two annual celebrations help to bring the ancient culture back to life. "Kids Day" in May features hands-on activities like pottery making, flint knapping, spear throwing, games, and face painting.

During September's "Heritage America," you'll see demonstrations of Indian dances, basket weaving, food preparation, and crafting of items from stone, bone, shell, and fiber.

Besides its reputation as a world-class archaeological site, Cahokia Mounds also represents an unsolved mystery. It seems nobody knows what became of this advanced ancient civilization. By A.D. 1500, less than 300 years after its zenith, Cahokia lay abandoned. What became of her people is unknown.

They just disappeared. Mysteriously. And without a trace.

Land of the Mound Builders

FOR MORE INFORMATION

There is a suggested admission donation for adults and children. For information about tours, lectures, seminars, and other special events, contact the Cahokia Mounds State Historic Site, Collinsville Road, Collinsville, IL 62234; (618) 346-5160.

22

Mozart Mania

WOODSTOCK

ORSON WELLES, WHO PLAYED HIS FIRST SHAKESPEAREAN ROLE in local theater here, called Woodstock the "grand capital of mid-Victorianism in the Midwest."

Bill Murray filmed several scenes from his *Groundhog Day* movie in and around the restored turn-of-the-century town square.

And square-jawed crime fighter Dick Tracy has "his" museum in a historic building in this quaint setting.

So while we're name-dropping like crazy, let's not forget Wolfgang Amadeus Mozart. Although the immortal composer never laid an eye on Woodstock (heck, the United States itself was only in its infancy when Wolfie died in 1791), this Victorian town has embraced the man and his music, showcasing his genius during its annual Woodstock Mozart Festival.

This summer extravaganza features three weekends of orchestral concerts (usually held in August) presented by some of the country's finest conductors and musicians. For example, one of the honored guests in previous years was Alan Balter, recognized by National Public Radio as "one of the three or four most important young conductors in America today." And the music included everything from symphonies and a divertimento to clarinet concertos.

Another interesting wrinkle is a chance to meet some of the musicians and conductors during preconcert "dialogues" and postconcert receptions. Tickets for these events must be purchased separately from concert series tickets.

But it's not just the music, conductors, and musicians that make Woodstock's Mozart Festival so special. All performances take place in the intimate, opulent 1889 Woodstock Opera House. This magnificently restored theater is an outstanding example of what's been called the "Steamboat Gothic" style of architecture: its exterior resembles that of a cathedral while the interior is similar to that of an ornate salon on a turn-of-the-century Mississippi River steamboat.

Especially note the intricately stenciled auditorium ceiling and the horseshoe balcony—just two outstanding features of this historic building.

Summer

And yes, you can buy a Mozart Festival T-shirt.

Besides the music, other aspects of Woodstock are worth exploring, since the town continues to exude oodles of Victorian charm. Boutiques, art galleries, and specialty shops inhabit restored turn-of-the-century buildings that surround the town square, which was first platted in 1844.

Noteworthy is the Old Courthouse Arts Center, a fine arts gallery located in that historic building listed on the National Register of Historic Places. And the Dick Tracy Museum features displays of comic strip drawings and prints created by the detective's mastermind, Chester Gould. You also can obtain a brochure (from the Chamber of Commerce office) that pinpoints self-guided tours of historic landmarks and period houses, some dating back to the 1860s.

If you're not going to this year's Mozart Festival, a great time to visit Woodstock is mid-August. That's when the annual Art Fair On-the-Square welcomes scores of the Midwest's best artisans as they display their creations in many media, including pottery, sculpture, paintings, and etchings.

You can even overnight in the historic town. Just a few blocks from the town square is the Bundling Board Inn, a

1910 Queen Anne–style bed and breakfast, furnished with Victorian antiques. And just outside town sits the Spring-Shire Inn, an elegant 1886 Italianate mansion boasting beautifully landscaped gardens and an in-ground swimming pool.

FOR MORE INFORMATION

For more Woodstock Mozart Festival information, contact the fest at (815) 338-5300; for Woodstock information, contact the Woodstock Chamber of Commerce, (815) 338-2436.

Mozart Mania

23

The Town That Time Forgot

GALENA

THESE DAYS, NO ONE IS FORGETTING "THE TOWN THAT TIME forgot."

About one million visitors annually pour an estimated $50–$70 million into Joe Daviess County. Galena, the famed 19th-century lead-mining boomtown known for its unique architectural heritage, art galleries, boutiques, restaurants, and bed and breakfasts, is responsible for most of that largesse.

Unlike many other small American towns, Galena's economy is growing; it enjoys nearly 100 percent occupancy of commercial buildings in its historic Main Street downtown business district; and it has a low unemployment rate. Its tough zoning and historic preservation ordinances keep it architecturally and historically "pure." Real estate prices are so high that they provide windfalls to those willing to sell property.

And the town has recently undergone a definite "upscaling" of many of its businesses—leading to even more hordes of spendthrift shoppers.

Quite simply, Galena is a modern-day boomtown going through the same process that occurred in its early days when lead was first discovered here. Only this time, it's tourists that are getting the lead out and transforming Galena into a gold mine.

In Illinois, only Springfield rates ahead of Galena in number of visitors per year (Chicago not included). How did all this happen?

Galena History

When miners discovered lead in the rolling hills of northwestern Illinois in the 1820s, Galena was born. Up until the end of the Civil War, the prosperous boomtown counted 16,000 residents while Chicago was just a tent town on a swamp. (This often-repeated historical tidbit is a favorite of Galena natives.)

Summer

Most Mississippi River traffic between Minnesota and St. Louis paused in Galena; sometimes nearly 20 riverboats docked at the Galena River levee at the same time.

U. S. Grant arrived on the steamboat *Itasca* in 1860 and made Galena his home. Not necessarily by choice, though. When he failed at other enterprises, Grant was sent by his father from Ohio to work in his brother's Galena leather goods store. Eventually he trained and mustered troops here before going off to fight in the Civil War.

Upon his return in 1865, a huge parade greeted the leader of the Union army with a massive reception at the DeSoto House, where today's visitors can still overnight in high style. They even gave him a modest brick house, now a state historic site open to visitors.

With railroads bypassing Galena and the silting of the river, the town experienced a decades-long depression following the Civil War. No one had money to either demolish or remodel buildings constructed during the town's bountiful years. It wasn't until the mid-1960s that Chicago artists discovered the wonders of Galena's architecture and small-town charm; they began purchasing historic buildings and restoring them.

And the boom was on!

Today nearly 85 percent of the town is listed on the National Register of Historic Places, including all of Main Street.

Main Street Shopping

The 10-block-long heart and soul of old Galena contains almost every kind of shop imaginable. And it's gone considerably upscale in the last few years, with high-quality art galleries, boutiques, and craft shops lining the historic Main Street.

The most unique specialty boutique might be You Gotta Be Kidding, offering everything from Chicago Cubs Christmas wreaths to personalized bronze busts by artist Charles Fach.

Banowetz Antiques is a browser's delight; best bet for Galena T-shirts—Honest John's Emporium and Trading Post; and the Kandy Kitchen's sinful creations are irresistible.

Among the galleries, The Friedl Collection is one of the classiest; housed in a pre–Civil War building on South Main, it's an unusual mixture of historic and contemporary works—many by Galena artists.

Architecture Tours

Even veteran Galena-goers will find the free slide show and exhibits at the Old Market Place House, once the hub of community life during the town's boom days, helpful in understanding its historic architecture.

Then pick up a brochure at the Depot Visitors Center in East Galena just across the bridge opposite Main Street) and hit the bricks for a self-guided walking tour of historic buildings. Two detailed routes (each taking about 45 minutes) cover 63 historic sites.

If you'd rather ride, narrated Galena trolley tours depart from 220 North Main daily on the hour. And if there are at least six persons in your group, you can book a one-hour tour of U. S. Grant's home and neighborhood with Grant impersonator Paul LeGreco.

Special Highlights

Here are some of the special highlights of Galena.

- Climb up the 212 steps from Main Street to High Street for a panoramic view of town.

- Tour the Toy Soldier Collection, a military miniatures shop on South Main owned by LeGreco. His handmade figures have been on display in the National Gallery in Washington, D.C., and range in price from $399 each to $1 for three Civil War soldiers.

- The award-winning video of Galena history shown hourly at the Galena/Jo Daviess County History Museum on South Bench Street shouldn't be missed.

- Jaekels' Bakerie & Cafe on South Main creates the best cinnamon rolls I've ever tasted.

- The Vinegar Hill Historic Lead Mine & Museum, six miles north of Galena on State 84, offers guided tours of an underground 1822 lead mine still in the hands of the founding family.

- Native Jim Post's one-man show, "Galena Rose," is a gem.

Bed and Breakfasts

With more than 40 bed and breakfasts, country inns, and historic hotels, Galena claims status as the country's B&B capital. Some of the best include the Aldrich Guest House, an 1853 Greek Revival mansion on whose lawn Gen. U. S. Grant once drilled his Civil War recruits; the DeSoto Hotel, the historic headquarters of Grant's 1868 presidential bid; Hellman Guest House, an 1895 Queen Anne mansion whose location (atop Horseshoe Mound) and top-floor turret room garner it the best steeple-top views of the entire town; the Queen Anne Guest House, an outstanding 1891 "Painted Lady"; and Pine Hollow Inn, a comfy inn nestled on a 110-acre Christmas tree farm less than two miles north of the downtown district; in fact, Pine Hollow sits on land once known locally as "Hughlett's Bottom." Imagine if the inn's owners had used that historical name for their place.

Restaurants

In the 1950s, Galena gourmet food might have consisted of a hamburger smothered with Velveeta. Not anymore—and casual attire reigns supreme even at the fanciest eatery.

For breakfast: try the Hobo Hash at the Farmers' Home Hotel; the Gold Room for great sausage; morning glory muffins at Baker's Oven; or grab a stool at the Steakburger Inn for inexpensive specials.

Lunchtime's best bets include pita sandwiches at Benjamin's or a one-third-pound Grant Burger at Grant's Place, where waitpersons dress in Civil War uniforms.

Recommended for dinner is the Cafe Italia, owned by a former Chicago cop; its Fettuccine Sardegna (Alfredo sauce and shrimp and scallops over pasta) is a winner. And Bubba's is a lot of fun.

Others swear by Silver Annie's pork chops and Log Cabin steaks (a local favorite).

For More Information

For more Galena area information, contact the Galena/Jo Daviess County Convention and Visitors Bureau, 101 Bouthillier Street, Galena, IL 61036; (800) 747-9377 or (815) 777-0203.

24

African American Legacies

IT SEEMS A SHAME THAT WE DESIGNATE ONLY ONE MONTH
out of the year to becoming more aware of contributions
made by African Americans and their legacies rather than
celebrating (or at least more visibly recognizing) these traditions year-round.

Filling this gap are a few Midwest states that have
recently published travelers' guides to African American heritage. Others are in the process of putting them together.
And some cities celebrate these roots with big-time African-
tinged festivals.

Illinois is home to some of the Midwest's most interesting African American historic sites and celebrations. In fact,
98 specific locations have been designated in its travelers'
guide to African American Heritage as superb starting points
for an adventure in discovery of the state's African American history. Some are open year-round, others have more
restricted schedules. Be sure to call ahead, confirming dates,
times, and admission fees. Here are some of the highlights.

- There's not much actually to "see," but it's worth noting
  that the **Jean Baptiste Pointe DuSable Home &
  Trading Post Site** marks the spot on which a Haitian
  immigrant became the first non-Indian settler in what is
  now Chicago. In 1779, DuSable located his trading post
  on the portage between the Chicago and Des Plaines
  Rivers. (This is now the heart of downtown Chicago, at

401 North Michigan Avenue, north of Wacker Drive.) Records show that his house measured about 22 feet by 40 feet and that he added several other buildings over time. His business attracted Indians and other traders, "establishing a pattern for the commercial city that would evolve during the following century." The site is listed on the National Historic Register of Historic Places.

Summer

- The **DuSable Museum of African American History**, opened in 1961, is the country's oldest African American repository highlighting a proud people's culture and achievement. Located at 740 East 56th Place in Chicago, it features more than 10,000 artifacts, photographs, art objects, and memorabilia telling the story of a people, and its collections include everything from African wood-carvings and ivory to slave documents and civil rights writings. The museum also sponsors special lectures, workshops, and African American history classes. Call (773) 947-0600.

- Tour the **Owen Lovejoy Homestead** in Princeton, which includes the restored wood-frame house where the nationally known abolitionist lived. In 1837, Lovejoy's brother Elijah was killed by a pro-slavery mob in southern Illinois; that brought him northward, where he assisted scores of escaped slaves on their journey to freedom, entered politics, and was elected to the state legislature. Later, he served five terms in the U.S. House of Representatives, introducing legislation that became a precedent for Lincoln's Emancipation Proclamation. Call (815) 879-9151.

- Springfield's **Old State Capitol** offers guided tours with costumed interpreters during "Mr. Lincoln's World," a special program (Fridays and Saturdays, except mid-April through May) that dramatizes racial and social tensions of the 1850s. Call (217) 785-7960.

- Slaves escaping to the North on the Underground Railroad were sheltered in the **Kinsey Crossing Farm**, located near Tamaroa. Evidence of the 1854 home's legacy was found in an attic strongbox, where papers and journals revealed that the farmstead's original Roots family hid slaves on several spots of the property. In fact, Roots became so unpopular for his slave-saving activities that he had to flee town on more than a few occasions to avoid a tar and feathering. It's also said that many slaves whom Roots saved returned here after the Civil War, building their own houses on land provided by Roots. Some of these African Americans are buried on the farm. Call (618) 496-3125.

- The **Black Pioneers Exhibit** at Alton's Museum of History and Art chronicles local and national African American history while focusing on abolitionist Elijah Lovejoy, early settlers, and black pioneers along the Mississippi River.

  There's also a unique video history program featuring local black residents and their remembrances of times past. Call (618) 462-2763.

- You'll need a good pair of hiking boots to slosh through the muck while reaching **Miller Grove Cemetery** in Golconda. It's the last vestige of an early African American settlement that some claim was the first "all-Negro" community in Illinois, established before the Civil War.

  Free black families came here in the 1830s, some burials date back to 1865, but everyone had deserted the "town" by 1925. Call (618) 949-3493.

- Walk among outdoor art exhibits at the **African American Heritage Museum and Black Veterans Archives** in Aurora. Guided tours, explaining the significance of sculptures created by Dr. Charles Smith, focus on works of art depicting the African homeland, the slave trade, and modern-day figures like Dr. Martin Luther King Jr. and Nelson Mandela.

- French settlers in what's been called Illinois's French Colonial district in **Cahokia** brought the first West Indian slaves into the region in the 1730s to work in lead mines. In fact, by 1732, Cahokia had 182 slaves—106 listed as "Negro" and 76 as "Indian." Caribbean slaves brought their culture with them, and in return for inhumane treatment allegedly poisoned some of their masters "using secret rituals of sorcery." Slaves who went on trial for these murders were indicted for witchcraft, not murder.

  Located behind the Church of the Holy Family, a large white cross designates the spot where some of the poisoned "victims" were buried. Slavery lingered in this area well into the 19th century. Call (618) 332-1782 or (618) 337-4548.

- Weekenders willing to take a short side trip north, about a half-hour past the Illinois-Wisconsin state line, can go to Milwaukee, which hosts two of the Midwest's biggest African American festivals. **Juneteenth Day**, scheduled for mid-June on Martin Luther King Drive, is said to have originated in Texas, where slaves didn't hear about the 1863 emancipation until after the Civil War. In fact, Texas farmers withheld news of the proclamation until June 19, 1865—after the harvest had been brought in by their "workers." The celebration begins with a parade and includes live ethnic music, dance, arts, crafts, and food.

- **African World Festival**, in August, is a massive celebration on the Summerfest lakefront grounds. Beginning with colorful opening ceremonies featuring the release of four white doves to symbolize the festival's blessing, the three-day bash offers all kinds of cultural excitements and reawakenings. For information about either celebration, call (800) 554-1448.

FOR MORE INFORMATION

You may still be able to get your hands on a copy of Illinois's 40-page black history guidebook called *Illinois Generations: A Traveler's Guide to African American Heritage*; otherwise, the Illinois Bureau of Tourism, (800) 223-0121, will have additional information.

African American Legacies

25

Illinois State Parks

MY FAMILY STOOD ATOP A STEEP BLUFF-TOP AERIE overlooking the mighty river at Mississippi Palisades State Park in the northwest corner of Illinois. We had scaled the tree-studded pinnacle to gaze across the swift-moving water and look over into Iowa.

"This is the biggest river I ever saw," said Kate, my then eight-year-old daughter. "My geography book says it's the biggest in the United States."

"Yeah, but I wouldn't want to swim across it," said Dayne, her younger sister, who was warily eyeing the rolling river. "I'd rather swim at the pool in our hotel."

Dayne has a good point. But we didn't come to swim the Miss'sip; we came to see the awesome beauty that's just a weekend road trip away at Illinois's state parks.

In fact, the state's 66 woodland wonderland preserves offer something for every member of the family: sweeping scenic vistas, historic places and traces, an abundance of wildlife and natural attractions, and almost unlimited recreational opportunities that include hiking, biking, fishing, swimming, and other outdoor fun.

And with a seven-year, $100 million expansion and renovation program completed a few years ago, Illinois's state parks can rightfully be called some of the finest in the Midwest.

Whether you're planning a day trip, weekend getaway, or week-long vacation, there's a state park that's right for you. And it's not just campers and RV enthusiasts who get to enjoy it all. With seven luxurious lodges sprinkled throughout the state park system, travelers can marvel at nature in first-class style, too.

Here are some of the finest Illinois state parks.

Starved Rock State Park   Canyons and waterfalls in the Midwest? Yep, and it's these fabulous formations that have transformed Starved Rock State Park into one of Illinois's most popular weekend destinations.

History and legend combine to make this 2,630-acre retreat along the Illinois River in Utica a year-long visitors' mecca. In fact, the park gets its name from a tale about a trapped band of Illiwek who were starved to death atop a 125-foot sandstone butte by warring rival tribes.

Eighteen canyons formed by the great glacial drift have transformed the flatland prairie into a geological wonderland. Naturalist-led spring and fall hikes explore remote corners of the park, while do-it-yourself trekkers can follow marked trails that reveal breathtaking canyon vistas sporting names like Lovers Leap and Sandstone Point.

The park's lodge emphasizes its Indian heritage by displaying its collection of Indian artifacts. Nowhere is this more evident than in the Great Room, with its freestanding fireplace surrounded by Native American handwoven rugs and original Indian art.

New guest rooms and cabin rooms tilt toward luxury, and the lodge's restaurant serves up such specialties as Linguine Alfredo with Clam Sauce.

Giant City State Park   Giant City State Park in Makanda is nestled amid the spectacular southern Illinois hardwoods of Shawnee National Forest. But these 3,700 Land of Lincoln acres are more like gardens of the gods, with massive sandstone bluffs and giant rock formations dwarfing trees and wildlife, and ancient Indian rock shelters dotting the aeons-old landscape.

Most incredible are towering stone walls that form narrow streetlike passages resembling a naturally formed "giant city." Hiking trails like the Devil's Standtable, Stonefort, and Indian Creek Shelter bring visitors to the brink of their high-country paradise; there's even a trail especially designed for visually impaired trekkers.

The bluff-top forests of Giant City also house shelter bluffs used by ancient inhabitants dating to 400 B.C. You can see the ceilings blackened from fires in two of these sheltered caves even today.

A 1930s-era lodge, fashioned with multihued sandstone and white oak timbers, provides handsome shelter for modern-day visitors. A massive stone Great Room resembles a feudal castle, and the Bald Knob dining room offers what's been called "the best fried chicken ever."

Three types of guest cabins are set in historic, prairie, and bluff-top surroundings (the bluff-top cabins have decks overlooking lush woods below).

Cave-in-Rock State Park   Until 1834, river pirates preyed on flatboat travelers plying the Ohio River from Cave-in-Rock, on Illinois's southeastern tip. Lured to the mouth of the den by signs proclaiming "Women, Whiskey and Entertainment," the unwary were robbed, or worse.

But after most of the outlaws had been captured or killed, the cave became a refuge for pioneers on their way to the Great Plains. In fact, Cave-in-Rock was a famous landmark shown on maps as early as 1744.

Today Cave-in-Rock State Park promises mystery, legend, and natural beauty, with 60-foot-high hills and rugged bluffs providing the 150-acre park with panoramic views of the Ohio. Four duplex guest houses have private balconies with river vistas. A family-style restaurant offers down-home specialties like Southern fried catfish and hush puppies.

Visitors should be sure to hike up the Pirates Bluff trail for a look at the original cave; or consider a boat ride down the Ohio for a perspective similar to that of early river travelers.

Illinois State Parks

White Pines State Park   White Pines State Park is located in the heart of the Rock River Valley. Nearby Mt. Morris is also Black Hawk Indian country, site of an 1834 Native American uprising that sent many white settlers scurrying back East. It also introduced a young Abraham Lincoln to military service.

It's easy to understand why Native Americans would fight for their homeland. Majestic white pines studded the landscape. Wildflowers bloom everywhere in season, with trout lily, Solomon's seal, bloodroot, and blue-eyed grass blossoming brightly. Vines trail from moss-covered limestone cliffs. And wildlife abounds.

The park's lush evergreen forests offer hiking trails skirting the famous Chicago-Iowa Trail, for years the main east-west route across northern Illinois; there's excellent bank fishing and remarkable peaceful camping. The inn features 25 one-room guest cabins—even a "Sweetheart" hideaway complete with a canopied waterbed.

Also try the inn's famous Paul Bunyan breakfast—bacon, sausage, toast, juice, coffee, and all you-can-eat pancakes and eggs. Be certain to visit the park's country store, full of handicrafts fashioned by local artists and supplies of delicious homemade fudge.

Illinois State Park in Zion   The deep blue water of Lake Michigan is the prime attraction at Illinois State Park in Zion. This northern Illinois haven has 6.5 miles of shoreline, sandy beaches, and great sunrises and sunsets.

Originally territory of the Algonquin Indian Nation and home to the peaceful Potowatomi tribe, the park's 4,160 acres are strewn with arrowheads, axheads, and other artifacts that bespeak their Native American origin.

Beachcombers marvel at more than three miles of sandy stretches, ideal for walking or jogging. These gentle dunes are part of a formation once stretching from south of Chicago to the Wisconsin state line. In fact, Illinois's only remaining sand dunes are within the park's boundaries.

Summer

The park's north section contains the North Point Marina, with room for 1,500 boats. And its hotel is a sleek, modern resort with handsome guest rooms, an Olympic-size indoor swimming pool, a massive whirlpool, and a full health club. Southern-style cooking reigns at the restaurant, with fried catfish a tasty specialty.

Pere Marquette State Park   Rolling bluffs just outside Grafton are the handsome setting for Pere Marquette State Park. Overlooking the Illinois River, this 8,000-acre retreat (named for French missionary Father Jacques Marquette, who paddled here in 1673 with fellow explorer Louis Jolliet) is a treasure trove of natural beauty.

The centerpiece of the park is its massive lodge, originally built in the 1930s by the Civilian Conservation Corps and recently renovated to a first-class facility. It has a distinctive flavor of native stone and rustic timbers, and the 700-ton stone fireplace in the Great Room is imposing and memorable. Guest rooms offer both bluff and river views.

Sunday brunch at the lodge draws people from all over Illinois and Missouri. Among the tastebud-tempting choices are fried chicken, pork chops, roast beef, and a mouthwatering dessert bar of fresh-baked goodies such as Amaretto cheesecake.

Eagle Creek State Park   Local Amish craftspeople have fashioned many furnishings for the Inn at Eagle Creek State Park. Huddled against the western shore of Lake Shelbyville in Findlay, this 2,147-acre resort is one of the Midwest's newest and most luxurious state park retreats.

Here country accents blend with European sensibilities. Guest rooms have countryside and lake views. A swimming pool and fitness center keep active guests happy even during inclement weather. And an 18-hole championship golf course is a duffer's paradise.

Illinois State Parks

The Wildflowers Dining Room serves fine cuisine in a casual atmosphere. Choose from Alaska salmon, Atlantic swordfish, lobster tail, or Dover sole meunière. And save room for a dessert of strawberries sabayon.

Mississippi Palisades State Park Mississippi Palisades State Park is rich in American Indian history. Its trails, especially the southern routes, trace the footsteps taken by Native American pathfinders. The 2,500-acre park, near where the Mississippi and Apple Rivers come together, is three miles north of Savanna.

Twin Sisters, a pair of humanlike figures on the bluff tops, and Indian Head are among the park's intriguing rock formations naturally carved by years of erosion. And the limestone caves at Palisades often plunge straight down.

The unique character of several other state parks makes them visitor favorites; these include Indian effigy mounds at Buffalo State Park in Ottawa; unspoiled pioneer prairie at Goose Lake Prairie State Park in Morris (a town that also claims the beginnings of the historic Illinois & Michigan canal); and spring and fall waterfowl migrations at Horseshoe Lake in Granite City.

FOR MORE INFORMATION

When planning a trip to one of the state parks listed above, be sure to call ahead for lodge rooms, cabins, and campground site reservations, if possible. Remember that space can fill up quickly, especially on holiday weekends and during the prime-time summer season.

For specific park information, call Cave-in-Rock State Park in Cave-in-Rock, (618) 289-4325; Eagle Creek State Park in Findlay, (217) 756-8260; Giant City State Park in Makanda, (618) 457-4836; Illinois Beach State Park in Zion, (847) 662-

Summer

4811; Pere Marquette State Park in Grafton, (618) 786-3323; Starved Rock State Park in Utica, (815) 667-4726; White Pines Forest State Park in Mt. Morris, (815) 946-3717.

For more Illinois state park information, contact the Illinois Bureau of Tourism, Department of Natural Resources, (217) 782-7454, and the Illinois Bureau of Tourism, (800) 223-0121.

Illinois State Parks

26

Corny Fun

I HOPE YOU'RE ALL EARS. OTHERWISE YOU'LL MISS OUT ON ALL the corny fun at this summer's sweet corn festivals.

Midwestern harvest hoopla demands homage to the corn crop. Illinois ranks second nationally for feed corn production. And Wisconsin, our neighbor to the north, places number two among sweet corn producers, according to recent agricultural statistics.

Since the Land of Lincoln is a kind of "corn king," it celebrates this kudo with lots of corny happenings. So jest set back a spell, ya hear, and enjoy the down-home shenanigans at Illinois's August and September corn fests.

Mendota You can sample some of the 50 tons of corn (about 160,000 ears) served free at the annual national Sweet Corn Festival in Mendota, a farming community about 80 miles west of Chicago. Served steaming hot from boilers heated by an antique steam engine and smothered in butter, the corn is usually dished up following the Sweet Corn Festival Mile Long Parade. Free music, a beer garden, and a corn-eating contest also are on tap. Mendota is on State 34, west of U.S. Route 39. For information, call (815) 539-6507.

Urbana The Sweet Corn Festival in Urbana expects hungry corn eaters to consume about 16,000 ears; you pay a negligible price for each ear. Corn is husked by hand and cooked in a giant antique steam engine.

Action takes place on Main Street between Race and Bennet, and on Broadway between Water and Elm, and includes live music, a corn-eating contest, games and entertainment like puppet shows and magicians, an arts-and-crafts show, and food booths offering beer, brats, and more. Kids receive free balloons, can explore an antique fire truck, and visit Sparky, the local fire department pooch. Urbana is 135 miles south of Chicago, off I-57. Call (800) 223-0121.

DeKalb　The DeKalb Corn Fest serves 16,000 free ears of corn during its late August bash. Weekend festivities center on an antique auto show, an art festival, free music stages, seven blocks of food booths, historic home tours (featuring the Ellwood House, whose namesake invented barbed wire), a 10k race, 2k walk, toddler trot, and diaper derby.

Wackiest offering is the corny cow contest, where for a 50-cent chance, you could win up to $500. Delicately put, a cow enters a fenced pastureland, whose area has been sectioned into identifiable checkerboard-like squares. The winner is determined by wherever she "plops" first. DeKalb is about 38 miles west of Chicago at the intersection of State 38 and 23. Call (815) 756-6306.

Hoopeston　Hoopeston's National Sweet Corn Festival, generally held over the Labor Day weekend, uses a 1910 Port Huron steam engine to cook its corn to perfection, then smothers it in butter. More than 25 tons will be served free. Saturday features a Grand Parade with more than 56 floats and marching bands that ends in McFarren Park, headquarters for the fest.

On Sunday, the National Sweetheart Pageant features runners-up from state Miss America contests in a beauty show that's considered to be a training ground for future beauty queens.

The fest also includes free concerts, kids' games, volleyball tournaments, and more; there is a nominal charge for some events. Hoopeston is 100 miles south of Chicago, off I-57 to Paxton, then east on State 9. Call (217) 283-7873.

FOR MORE INFORMATION

For other corn festival information, contact the Illinois Bureau of Tourism, (800) 223-0121.

Corn Fun

27

Garfield Farm

LAFOX

HAVE YOU EVER SEEN A PINK TOMATO WITH WHITE STRIPES? How about a green melon dotted with half-moons and stars? Or eggplants that are not only white but almost the exact shape of eggs?

Can you imagine an early 1800s carrot more than a foot and a half long? Or purple tomatoes? Or blue potatoes?

Well, seeing (and tasting) is believing. And picking through all kinds of antique vegetables, fruits, exotic edible plants, and historic flowers is what makes the Garfield Farm Museum's annual Heirloom Garden Show so much fun.

Every August, nearly 20 growers exhibit all kinds of old goodies on the grounds of the rural Kane County museum's historic 1840s New Englander farmstead (that also encompasses outbuildings and a teamster inn); only here will you understand how produce got exotic names like Jacob Cattle, Salts Cave, Atlantic Giant, and King of the Garden.

You'll even be able to see plants and order seed to grow the same kinds of flowers that Thomas Jefferson planted in his garden at Monticello.

This is the only Midwest show of the Seed Savers Exchange (SSE), a national nonprofit group working to save the genetic diversity of domestic plants. The exchange identifies individuals growing antique fruits and vegetables not available on the commercial market and helps save the seeds.

It's an important task because the United States national seed bank is quite limited. For example, only 150 of the 530 varieties of tomatoes known to the SSE are currently in the national seed bank.

You'll meet all kinds of antique goodies (carrots, cabbages, melons, corns, beans, squashes, eggplants, cucumbers, tomatoes, horseradish, hot peppers, shallots, and more) at Saturday's bash.

"Tomatoes can be real crowd pleasers," said Jerome Johnson, executive director of the museum. "People might be surprised to learn that they come in all colors—from reds and yellows to oranges and purples.

"Shapes vary, too," he added. "Some look more like peaches, others are ribbed rather than smooth. There are even some that resemble berries, no more than a half-inch in diameter."

You'll see a curious corn pod plant, with each individual kernel housed in its own husk. It dates to prehistory.

Some growers may even exhibit everything from onions, shallots, and garlic plants to the wild leek, the once-prolific and odorous plant that gave Chicago (a variation of an Indian word meaning "bad smell") its name.

Even the common bean can be pretty interesting. Especially when you're looking at Jacob Cattle beans, which are white with purplish spots ("making them colorful like the coat worn by Joseph in the Old Testament," Johnson said). And take a close look at the soldier bean, which exhibits a silhouette of a soldier carrying a rifle.

Johnson noted that it's important for growers to save plant varieties not only for historical preservation but for practical reasons.

"Today, farmers are under pressure to grow only one or two varieties of a commercial crop that are most profitable," he said. But recent reports reveal that a fungus similar to the one that attacked potatoes in 1840s Europe is resurfacing in the United States, and sometimes not responding to "regular" fungicides, he added.

"So resistance to certain blights in unused plant varieties might be needed to protect certain crops somewhere in the future."

Ravages from crop diseases, like the 19th-century Irish potato blight that resulted in over one million deaths from starvation, are just one of the reasons to encourage the genetic diversity of our plants. Who knows what plants might be needed by scientists for future medical treatment or nutritional improvements.

The Seed Savers Exchange is a way that backyard gardeners can help with this task.

At the show, you can order seeds for heirloom fruits and vegetables (that will become available between January and May) to grow in your own garden.

Some heirloom produce will be on hand for sale. And there'll be an antique flower garden and demonstration prairie plot on display.

One exhibit I found fascinating featured a Michigan grower who claimed to have grown tomatoes from four seeds found in the 4,000-year-old Egyptian tomb of the pharaoh Os-Oh-Pe-L. He offered seeds for sale that he claims are direct descendants.

"It's especially interesting because the tomato is a plant of the Americas," Johnson said.

Does that mean the ancient Egyptians sailed to America thousands of years before Columbus?

"Well, it's a perfect example of interesting folklore and legends that sometimes add mystery to our accepted cultural traditions," Johnson said.

If you can't make Garfield Farm's show, there's still time to visit the Seed Savers Exchange Heritage Farm, located about 5.5 miles north of Decorah, Iowa. The two-acre preservation plot holds hundreds of antique tomato, bean, potato, and other vegetable and fruit varieties.

Free maps are available for self-guided walks through the farm. People are on hand to answer any questions you might have about the historic plants. For more information on this organization, write to the Seed Savers Exchange, 3076 North Winn Road, Decorah, IA 52101.

If you're not into veggies, note that Garfield Farm Museum offers special events throughout the year. One of the most popular is the Rare Breeds Livestock Show, held in mid-May, which features all kinds of farmstead animals typical to pioneer times, but quite unusual to modern eyes.

And then there's Prairie Walk days, slated at various times from late spring to late summer; they feature naturalist-led treks onto the farm's 20 acres of prairie left untouched by farm plow or land development schemes, so the landscape appears today much as it did more than 150 years ago.

It's likely that you won't even know the names of the plants and grasses in this prairie preserve simply because most of them are now extremely rare or simply no longer exist elsewhere.

"We've identified more than 125 native Illinois species of plants to date," said executive director Johnson. "And it seems more rare plants reappear every year due to the farm's restoration and management techniques."

During the three-hour-long guided prairie walk, Johnson identifies rare plants like Jacob's ladder, buttercups, wild geraniums, May apple, and scores of other wildflowers and grasses that started their decline with the opening of the prairie to agriculture in the mid-18th century.

He also explains the history of this precious prairie patch, challenging the notion that pioneers found "virgin prairie." In fact, this land had been occupied for nearly 8,000 years by native peoples before the onset of European-American settlers.

During spring walks, visitors will see scores of blossoming flowers like the Iowa crab, the Midwest's only native crab apple tree that sprouts pink blossoms through mid-

May. They'll also enjoy sweet fragrance like mountain mint, though some patches of wild leek give off a pungent odor that leaves no doubt what the Indians meant by the word *chicagou*—loosely translated as "bad smell."

In the dog days of summer, tall prairie grasses can reach heights of nearly nine feet while blooming flowers provide patches of color. And you've never seen sunflowers like these—10 to 12 feet tall topped by delicate blossoms no more than 4 inches in diameter.

Johnson also notes that the prairie's natural diversity suffered greatly with the onset of modern agriculture. At a demonstration plot near the 1840 house, a combination of fruits, vegetables, and grasses is rich with life, even drawing scores of butterflies.

"Then look at a two-acre field of hay or corn and compare," he said. "You'll see those plots are almost devoid of life."

Garfield Farm

For More Information

An admission fee is charged for all shows. Three-hour prairie walks usually begin early morning; reservations are necessary.

General tours of the 1840s homestead are offered June through September, on Sunday and Wednesday afternoons; all other times (year-round), by appointment only.

Garfield Farm is located in Lafox, about five miles west of Geneva, off State 38 on Garfield Road. For more information, contact Garfield Farm Museum, 3N016 Garfield Road, Lafox, IL 60147; (630) 584-8485.

28

Canoe Illini

NORTHERN ILLINOIS

IT WASN'T THE COVERED WAGON THAT OPENED UP EXPANSION
and settlement in North America.

Think canoe.

For thousands of years before the arrival of white European settlers, Native Americans paddled birchbark canoes
along continental river routes for trade and travel. Then
came early French explorers searching a vast "wilderness" in
arduous expeditions. They were followed by trappers and
traders, who set up beaver and otter lines and established
trading posts along rivers and streams that carried an
increasing amount of canoe traffic.

Sort of like permanently soggy expressways.

These days, weekenders use modern canoes (made of
everything from aircraft-quality aluminum to fiberglass) to
capture the same spirit of those early adventurers. In fact,
the varied topography of Illinois's waterways provides all
kinds of canoe fun—whether it be shooting white-water
rapids or lazily floating down a glass-smooth river close to
mighty bluffs.

And you don't have to travel very far into the "wilderness" to experience canoe adventures. Scenic waters and
riverfront beauty are only a few hours' drive from downtown Chicago.

"The northern third of Illinois has the prettiest rivers, anyway," says Ralph Frese, owner of the Chicagoland Canoe Base in Chicago, which rents outfitting gear to canoeist wanna-bes. "You've got dramatic sandstone bluffs, virgin pine forests, rolling countryside, and rare plant and animal communities all along these rivers."

More than 20 years ago, Frese reenacted the discovery of Illinois by tracing the expeditions of Jolliet and Marquette, alerting the nation to the debt we owe our canoeing voyageurs. Now he runs his outfitting shop, plans trips for canoeists, and builds historical canoe reproductions by hand. He's also one of the country's leading canoe gurus.

"What we try to do for people," he says, "is help them appreciate their trip by providing local color and history. Instead of having a boat ride, they get an adventure."

Here are some suggested waterways near the Chicago area just right for weekend canoe outings.

Illinois-Michigan Canal

It's especially beautiful here in the spring, with redbud trees and wildflowers blossoming along the banks. Start your float from Channahon State Park (about seven miles south of Joliet off U.S. Route 6 near the town of Channahon) and continue to Gebhard Woods, near Seneca, for a two-day trip.

The route exposes you to the Kankakee bluffs, and if you go ashore and climb to the top of the outcropping, the view is dramatic. The DuPage, Des Plaines, and Kankakee Rivers all come together at this point, giving birth to the Illinois River.

Frese says that the canal is one of the few waterways where you can make a round-trip if you plan correctly. Launch right where the dam is located in Channahon in the DuPage River, paddle down to the Des Plaines, and go down the Grand Creek cutoff, which takes you into the Kankakee River. Then make a right-hand turn at the mouth of the Kankakee where it joins the Des Plaines to the Dresden Lock and Dam on the Illinois; behind the dam make a 50-foot portage into the Illinois-Michigan Canal.

It will take you right back to where you started from on the DuPage.

Kishwaukee River

Northwest of Chicago, at the first Rockford exit on I-90, you cross the river. The small town of Cherry Valley is just south of the ramp. You can launch your canoe and float down to Milford, about a 10-mile journey, or paddle a few miles farther to the banks of the Rock River.

The Kishwaukee is an excellent fishing stream, according to Frese. Smallmouth bass, walleye, and northern pike can be found in abundance. "A friend of mine caught a two-and-a-half-pound trout here, of all places," Frese says. The trip is especially beautiful in early spring, with lush green countryside.

Fox Valley Canoe Trail

The Lower Fox, a 35-mile stretch south from Yorkville (about 12 miles southwest of Aurora), is perhaps the most scenic historic stretch of river in northern Illinois. It's a two-day journey, during which canoeists are treated to the most interesting collection of rare plants and animals to be found in any similar stream in the state, according to Frese.

Scenery is similar to the Wisconsin Dells, yet it's only an hour and a half from downtown Chicago. Bluffs 140 feet high line the river, with five varieties of native Illinois evergreens—plus the only native red pines (six of them) left in the state. Caves and caverns dot the riverscape, and signs of beaver and deer are everywhere. Hundreds of wildflowers are in spring bloom.

Rock River

Take North Avenue (State 64) west about 100 miles from Chicago to Oregon, and launch below the dam. Frese suggests floating down to Grand Detour, which he calls one of the most scenic 10-mile stretches in the state. The route is known as the "thousand island" section, but Frese says he has counted only 889. You'll find sandstone bluffs, beautiful pine forests, and unusual plant life supported by the sand country.

For a break, stop at the village of Grand Detour and visit the historic John Deere Museum, then begin your journey upstream. There is a quaint restaurant named Maxon's right on the riverbank nearing Oregon. It's a come-as-you-are spot serving down-home meals, a good place to visit before the long trip home.

Vermillion Middle Fork

From Potomac (about 35 miles northeast of Urbana on U.S. Route 136) to Kickapoo State Park, you may be astonished by a shoreline filled with wildlife and rare plants. There are five natural prairies, 243 species of birds, the state's largest concentration of wild orchids, a 50-foot active beaver dam, and Indian mounds and burial sites, along with more than a hundred archaeological digs.

It is a wild-looking, narrow river valley, with 90-foot bluffs and a few water ripples. Tulip trees 50 to 80 feet tall are in blossom in spring, and a second day's journey down the river to the south fork will float you into the town on Danville. Look out for sandbars near Salt Creek junction.

Another option is to spend a second day exploring the area's very deep strip-mining lagoons. Many of them are connected by shore channels or short portages.

Hennepin Canal

This is one of the finest examples of the country's canal-boat era, although it was obsolete before completion because its locks were too small to accommodate larger barges. However, it remains an interesting waterway, located about 110 miles southwest of Chicago, near Peru. In lovely countryside, it follows Big Bureau Creek (itself an interesting creek to float in the spring); it's a 15-mile trip between State 6 and 29. Remember, you're paddling upstream, and you'll have to portage up 15 old and inoperable canal locks.

Kankakee River

LaSalle explored this river in 1679; it is wide open, with bayous and marshes near the Indiana border. Orville Reed, of Reed's Canoes in Kankakee, is the outfitter for this area. Reed's operation offers several different river tours, lasting from three hours to three days. Rare mallow blossoms come to life in July near the confluence of the Kankakee River and Rock Creek. In August, golden locusts grow wild along the river's lower reaches. Avoid tricky navigation near the Wilmington Dam by using the millrace channel on the right bank.

Three "Bonus" Rivers

The Mackinaw River is a rural countryside stream with some high bluffs scuffing its banks. One spot is called the "Dells of the Mackinaw" because of its stone outcroppings. Launch below U.S. Route 51, south of Kappa (about 130 miles southwest of Chicago, 18 miles west of I-55); the trip takes a day. Swallow nesting sites can be seen, but expect portaging during low-water season.

The Des Plaines River from the Wisconsin state line to the city is another waterway worth exploring. An annual Canoe Marathon takes place on this river, usually in May.

Finally, the North Branch of the Chicago River can provide delightful canoeing, says Frese. The Skokie Lagoon itself contains water enough for a seven-mile trip. But you can launch below the main control dams at Willow Road and make a one-day trip through Harms Woods and Morton Grove into Caldwell Woods. Frese says that he has even traveled all the way into downtown Chicago on the river. But a trip like that is best left to experts.

FOR MORE INFORMATION

Always wear life jackets and follow safety standards during your canoeing adventures. Inexperienced canoers should sign up for paddling lessons, or at least tackle "beginner streams" before moving on to more advanced waterways. For rentals, detailed information, and maps of navigable rivers and streams in Illinois, and booklets on canoeing and canoe safety, contact:

Summer

Chicagoland Canoe Base, Ralph Frese, 4019 North Narragansett Avenue, Chicago, IL 60634-1599; (773) 777-1489. His outfitting store rents 17-foot aluminum canoes both daily and for weekends. Accessories included are car-top carriers, life jackets (mandatory), and paddles. Information about your river trip and tips on planning are freely given.

Reed's Canoe Trips, (815) 939-0053. Reed specializes in trips on the Kankakee and Iroquois Rivers. Three-hour to three-day trips are offered. Prices include a 17-foot aluminum canoe, life jackets, paddles, and transportation to and from the launch site.

Or contact the Illinois Bureau of Tourism, (800) 223-0121.

Canoe Illini

Fall

29

Apple Adventures

WAUCONDA

"HERE'S A GOOD ONE, PA!" SHOUTS KATE, MY OLDEST daughter. "It's shiny and red and perfect."

I walk over to the tall tree where Kate is trying to snare a huge Red Delicious apple near the top with her "picker"— a contraption that looks like a long broom handle with a little pouch attached to the end that snatches the apple off the tree without harming the limb.

Dayne, her sister, comes over to supervise the activity. But as Kate and I attempt to get that special apple, we shake some branches and a downpour of Red Delicious rains down on Dayne's noggin.

"Why can't you guys pick apples from the bottom of the trees like Mama and I do?" asks Dayne, rubbing her head as she speaks. "Then nobody would get their brains hurt."

That said, we all break out in laughter, and after a few hugs all around, return to our apple-pickin' ways.

In fact, apple picking is one family tradition that we've never broken. We get out in the country, breathe crisp fall air, nibble on some fresh apples, bring some home for delicious homemade pies, and spend some quality time with each other.

Life doesn't get much better than that.

Our favorite Illinois "U-pick" apple hot spot is Wauconda Orchards, boasting more than 10,000 apple trees spread over

250 acres. The Breeden family's farm has been a favorite fall weekend destination for years. It specializes in four apple varieties:

- McIntosh—tart and juicy, great for sauces and pies. Early-variety picking begins early September; regular McIntosh picking begins mid-September.

- Jonathan—very juicy with a touch of tartness, good for eating, taffy apples, pies, and salads. Picking begins mid-September.

- Red Delicious—the king of the apple family is sweet and juicy and keeps well in the refrigerator. Picking begins the last week in September.

- Golden Delicious—oblong, with green and red blushes, it's an all-purpose apple good for eating off the tree, sauces, and pies. Picking begins in early October.

Consider trying two other orchard varieties: the Idared, a cousin to Jonathan, is crisp, juicy, and a good keeper; the Rome Beauty is a terrific baking apple that keeps its big, round shape after a stint in the oven.

But it's not just apples that draw thousands of U-pick fruit lovers here.

Each apple-picking weekend at Wauconda Orchards features all kinds of fun. Kids can take a pony ride and pet a baby calf, bunnies, ducks, and other farm animals at the 4-H petting zoo. Climb into a pumpkin patch and pick out their jack-o'-lantern to be. Or hop aboard a horse-drawn hay-wagon for rides through the orchard's backwoods.

Moms and Dads can enjoy old-fashioned grilled sausage and sweet corn chased by a cold beer while listening to live country music and oompaa bands.

And post-picking headquarters remains the orchard's country store, featuring all kinds of down-home goodies and gadgets. Free samples on weekends include cheeses, sausage, homemade jams and preserves, and honey made from the farm's own beehives.

You also can pick up a plastic jug of "Old Rick" apple cider, one of the best-tasting concoctions around; sample delicious homemade apple-cinnamon doughnuts at the snack shop—we wolf down a half-dozen right on the spot, then buy another dozen for home treats; and you can purchase that "apple gizmo" here—a weird-looking hand-cranked device that decores and peels apples almost effortlessly, and really works!

Don't forget to visit the orchard's craft barn, stuffed with endless Halloween and Christmas goodies.

For More Information

U-pick apples are sold by half-bushel bags; picking poles are provided free of charge. Prepicked apples are also available in half-bushel bags. Seniors over 60 get 10 percent off apples every Wednesday. Wauconda Orchards does not use the chemical Alar on its fruit crops. The orchard is located on Gossell Road, just north of State 176 and Fairfield Road; it's about 60 miles northwest of Chicago. For more information, contact Wauconda Orchards, 1201 Gossell Road, Wauconda, IL 60084; (800) 362-7753 or (847) 526-8553.

Apple Adventures

30

Fall Color Caravan

LOOKING FOR THOSE PERFECT FALL COLORS, A BLAZING cacophony of fiery red maples, orangy sumacs, golden oaks, and burgundy ash trees?

Well, leaf peepers searching for Illinois's best autumn hues don't have to look very hard, thanks to hundreds of acres of tree-studded preserves in federal-, state-, and privately protected forests, parks, natural areas, wildlife reserves, bogs, marshes, and trails.

These precious preserves pretty much guarantee an annual cavalcade of color for many generations to come—as long as Mother Nature's weather whimsies don't throw the entire color cycle out of whack. And let's not forget other public lands, private holdings, and country lanes where blasts of color can be found.

All you have to remember are general guidelines for Illinois's fall color schedule: it begins in the state's far north climes (like Galena and Rockton) around mid- to late September, then works its way toward southern Illinois, where late autumn hues sometimes linger into late October. For prime Land of Lincoln colors at locations in between, figure mid-October and plan accordingly.

Here are some of Illinois's best fall color hot spots.

Little Black Slough For fall color like you've probably never seen before, head to Little Black Slough's cypress swamp, part of the Cache River State Natural Area near Karnak. Resembling Georgia's Okefenokee and Florida's Everglades, the 6,000-acre swamp is dotted with an almost impenetrable stand of 1,000-year-old bell-bottomed bald cypress trees; it also includes tupelo, oak, and maple forests (which add gold and crimson fall colors to the swampy palette), as well as prairie glades.

You can hike nine miles of trails here. One of the best is the Heron Pond Trail, leading into the heart of this primeval wilderness. You're likely to see all kinds of color and wildlife, including great blue herons and bald eagles. Stay on the path: there are lots of snakes around (poisonous water moccasins), but they usually avoid confrontations with humans.

Especially enticing are four-foot-wide floating boardwalks that literally allow you to walk on water—water that boasts a striking lime green surface color from swamp duckweed. Eerie and beautiful at the same time, the swamp is a sight you surely won't ever forget. Call (618) 634-9678.

Wildlife Prairie Park   A 2,000-acre zoological park west of Peoria that's home to animals that roamed Illinois during pioneer days, Wildlife Prairie Park is one of the best-kept fall-color secrets in the state.

Color explodes as you trek over nine trails, some passing huge natural habitat enclosures featuring wolves, bison, black bear, elk, cougar, waterfowl, and more. Other trails explore the park's spectacular natural settings, which include restored prairie, hardwood forests, tree-surrounded lakes, and butterfly gardens—all ablaze with more fall colors.

Hike to the park's pioneer area for tours of a 19th-century log cabin homestead and an 1850 one-room schoolhouse; kids love to pet the domesticated prairie farm animals. And if all this walking seems a bit much, just hop aboard the Prairie Railroad, which takes a relaxing chug through the wildlife park (it's a sister park to Chicago's Brookfield Zoo).

You can even overnight here, renting the "cabin on the hill" or a train caboose complete with "jiggler switch" that simulates rides over the rails. Call (309) 676-0998.

Shawnee National Forest Perhaps the Midwest's greatest combination of fall colors and natural wonders can be found in southern Illinois's Shawnee National Forest, 260,000 acres of ever-changing foliage that frames spectacular rock formations and oddities of nature carved by massive ice blocks of the last great glacier more than 10,000 years ago.

Headquartered in Harrisburg, the Shawnee boasts an amazing amalgam of wonders. Don't miss the Garden of the Gods, where easy-walking flagstone paths wind through a maze of towering rock formations nearly two million years old; many have been endowed with colorful names like Fat Man's Squeeze, Chimney Rock, and Noah's Ark.

For hiking among sheer cliffs, hulking boulders, and a winding canyon pocked with Indian caves, head to Bell Smith Springs. Not only is the springs area dusted with autumn hues, but downstream is a natural stone bridge, whose 125-foot-long arch curves 30 feet at its highest point.

Hardcore trekkers might challenge the Lusk Creek Canyon Trail. You'll be rewarded with incredible fall-color views at a 70-foot-high rock shelf called Indian Kitchen, but only after you've mastered a narrow wall-clinging trail to get there. Call (618) 253-7114 or (800) 526-1500.

River Valleys and State Parks In iffy fall weather (remember that leaves need warm days and cool nights, with no frosts, heavy rains, or driving winds, to produce good hues), color experts from the state's Department of Conservation suggest that leaf peepers keep to the river val-

Fall Color Caravan

leys for the best hues—especially around the Rock River near Oregon, the Illinois River near Springfield, and along the Great River Road that follows the Mississippi.

Another suggested strategy is to visit state parks like Starved Rock in Utica, Mississippi Palisades in Savanna, Giant City near Makanda, and Pere Marquette in Alton, which generally offer the best prospects for "pleasing colors" in even crummy color-producing weather.

U.S. Route 20 West One of the best fall-color roadways is U.S. Route 20 west, from Marengo toward Galena. Fire-red maples, black oak, hickory, and sweetgum trees blaze with autumn hues; and the closer you get to the Mississippi River near Galena (especially upon entering Jo Daviess County), the more you're rewarded with wide-angle views of layered and rolling hills, along with bluff-top color grandeur.

Another good color route is along the Knox County Scenic Drive on State 180, from Nauvoo to Hamilton. Historic towns along the road celebrate autumn during this two-weekend "drive party" in early October with all kinds of festivals, parades, craft shows, and special events. Same goes for the Spoon River Fall Festival, along U.S. Route 24, State 9, and south of London Mills on roads following the river. Here you can follow the woodsy landscape that inspired Edgar Lee Masters's *Spoon River Anthology*.

Ferne Clyffe State Park For unusual fall color, visit Ferne Clyffe State Park, south of Marion. Prickly ferns aren't the only attraction here—you'll discover beech, dogwood, gum, maple, sumac, oak, and ash trees ablaze in autumn hues. The effect is glorious, especially in the midst of Ferne Clyffe's canyons, gorges, glens, domes, creeks, rills, and other unique formations—like an intermittent waterfall 10 stories tall and a 150-foot-long shelter bluff called Hawk's Cave.

FOR MORE INFORMATION

For up-to-date fall color information, call the Illinois state hotline, (800) 624-3077, which offers color reports beginning in late September/early October. Other fall color touring information can be obtained by contacting the Illinois Bureau of Tourism, (800) 223-0121.

Fall Color Caravan

31

Jackpot Journeys

LESS THAN 20 MINUTES INTO THE INAUGURAL CRUISE OF THE
Casino Rock Island (which set sail in 1992), a glassy-eyed gen-
tleman bemoaned more than $300 in blackjack losses.

"I hate when that happens," he muttered. Then he pulled
a wad of bills nearly three inches thick from his pants
pocket, peeled off $20, and laid it on the green felt in front
of him to buy more chips.

"What the hell, might as well try it again," he said to the
dealer.

His never-say-die reaction is pretty typical, evidenced by
the soaring revenues that riverboat gambling is generating.
In fact, unlimited high-stakes casino boat wagering is a fever
sweeping America, and nowhere is the epidemic more evident than in Illinois.

Since the *Alton Belle* launched gaming on the state's waterways on April Fools' Day of 1991, more than 21 million passengers have spent (lost) more than $1.1 billion on Illinois's
gaming vessels. As of this writing, the Land of Lincoln
boasts a floating gold-mine fleet of casinos that gobble up
bets on blackjack, craps, slot machines, and other assorted
wagering faster than Honest Abe could split rails.

What's the attraction? The lure of the "big payoff." Like
the one that Bloomington roofing contractor David Riddle
collected after playing the "Big Hit" $1 progressive slot
machine on East Peoria's *Par-a-Dice*; feeding the machine for

only 15 minutes, he hit the jackpot—a whopping $479,147. That total remains America's largest riverboat casino payoff.

And it's that illusion of big money that is expected to continue to draw more passengers to the state's 13 boats than the combined attendance of ALL the state's professional and major-college sporting events.

So if you're into gambling big-time, or would like to see what all this riverboat casino stuff is about, here's a brief rundown on the state's ever-growing fleet.

Casino Rock Island   This boat sails on the Mississippi River out of its namesake Quad Cities port and is clearly the class of the fleet. It's pure Mark Twain–era riverboat nostalgia, a 220-foot-long, four-deck behemoth with gorgeous woodwork, red-shaded Victorian lamps, gold fixtures, etched glass, tin ceilings, and faux velvet wall coverings.

More than 600 passengers can squeeze onto its decks, and its gambling pits include 371 slot machines and 17 blackjack tables. There are free snack buffets on each deck, and a Dixieland trio plays enthusiastically at stations throughout the ship. You'll even find boarding the boat a pleasant experience in nostalgia, as you walk through three old river vessels before reaching the wagering playground.

Grand Victoria Casino   Another boat is the *Grand Victoria Casino*, a 400-foot-long, 100-foot-wide monster that floats on the Fox River out of Elgin. Opened in October 1994, it can hold up to 1,200 passengers—plenty enough to crowd around more than 1,000 slot machines, plus scores of other wagering games.

What makes the *Grand Victoria* so special is its single deck—strikingly different from any of the other currently operating casino boats. Architecturally, both the ship and its pavilion are a mixture of Victorian, Prairie, and casino styles. And it is the riverboat closest to the city of Chicago, which has yet to receive the go-ahead from state government for its own eagerly anticipated riverboat casino fleet.

Still, the developers are hedging their bets on repeat gamblers by developing a riverside pavilion that will include three movie theaters, two restaurants, a sports bar, and banquet facilities.

Alton Belle   Has anyone seen Elvis? It's Las Vegas gone amuck on the *Alton Belle*, Illinois's first floating casino. (Actually, it's a new boat with a contemporary design, traded for the original paddlewheeler.) The Caesar's Palace meets the Munsters motif includes "180,000 antique glittering Roman lights, art gallery with stone bas-relief, bronze statuary," and more. In fact, don't get startled when you're greeted on the main deck by a statue of Hercules wielding a club, with a lion and dog resting at his feet.

Players Riverboat Casino   Remember Merv Griffin? He owns the *Players Riverboat Casino*, a $7.5 million Hollywood-Victorian craft that sets sail in Metropolis (Superman's hometown, by the way). His silky, carnival barker's voice even makes a recorded pitch for some fun: ". . . so come on board and forget your worries for a while," Merv purrs.

The 210-foot-long, 1,400-passenger ship ventures out on the Ohio River from "Merv Griffin's Landing" (why be modest when you're rich?) in glitzy show-biz style, offering 634 slots, 28 blackjack tables, 4 craps tables, 2 roulette wheels, a "Big Six" wheel, and scores of video poker games spread over three decks.

I liked the landing better than the boat. Its Celebrity Buffet restaurant (low-priced roast beef and prime rib specialties, just like Vegas) is likened to a "tour through a Hollywood time capsule." That's because the walls are plastered with scores of photographs from Griffin's years as a talk show host. The montage of images includes everyone from Queen Elizabeth II to Cher.

There's also Merv's Bar & Grill. It sports a 40-foot-long solid mahogany bar and a wall of windows overlooking the river.

But the biggest attraction here? One account stated that "it's a bit shocking in this Bible Belt setting [the extreme tip of southern Illinois] to observe that the costumes of *Players'* cocktail waitresses show off more cleavage than on any boats in the state's bigger Sin Cities."

City of Lights I and II *City of Lights I* and *II* in Aurora are owned by Hollywood Casino, so there's a distinctive, mon-eyed La-La-Land flair to the surroundings. In the Fox Pavil-ion, which leads to the boats, movie memorabilia displays include Madonna's baseball glove used in the filming of *A League of Their Own*. A steak-and-lobster combination dinner at one of the boats' upscale restaurants will set you back almost $60 a plate. And some slot machines on the *City of Lights II* are marked "Accepts bills—$10, $20, $50—no need to waste time getting change." Its nearby Paramount Arts Theatre (an elegantly restored venue) presents big-name Hollywood acts like Liza Minnelli, Tom Jones, and more.

Par-a-Dice Located in East Peoria, *Par-a-Dice* is the big daddy of the big payoffs. Its Big Hit slots start with a jack-pot of $100,000 and swell until someone . . . well, hits it big. (Like the previously mentioned David Riddle, who cashed in to the tune of almost $500,000 on a $1 bet.) Count on more slots, video poker, keno (I still can't figure out how to play that game!), blackjack, roulette, craps, mini-baccarat, and more.

The Casino Queen Out of East St. Louis, the *Casino Queen* has never grabbed my fancy. Maybe it's just too darned big—this floating four-deck behemoth can carry almost 3,000 passengers on its Mississippi River cruises. Maybe it's just too loud for me; noise levels can be almost deafening. But the views across the river to St. Louis and the Gateway Arch are nice enough.

Fall

Northern Star and Southern Star   The Joliet area, about an hour's drive south of Chicago, beckons to gamblers with four riverboat casinos. Harrah's *Northern Star* and *Southern Star* offer great food—especially in Andreotti's, their pavilion restaurant. The yachtlike *Northern Star*, older of the two boats, offers free business people's cruises Monday through Thursday. It also contains a three-story atrium complete with fake clouds and sky. The *Southern Star*, a mock paddlewheeler design, also has a tall atrium.

Empress I and II   The *Empress I* and *II* have been called the biggest cash collectors among the Illinois riverboat casinos.

All these profits have been plowed back into the operation in the form of a new $40 million "palace," a pharaoh-themed pavilion that contains two sit-down restaurants and a food court. There's even an off-track betting facility (for horseplayers) already open on the premises.

Empress II offers craps and blackjack lessons on its top interior deck during certain days of the week. *Empress I* issues a key-club card (like a charge card) that can be used by frequent bettors to activate slot machines without dirtying their hands with cold cash.

But the best thing about sailing on a Joliet boat might be witnessing the "ballet of Joliet bridges." That's what happens when two of these boats pass each other on the Des Plaines River, requiring two small drawbridges to be raised in perfect synchronization.

151

Jackpot Journeys

For More Information

For more information about Illinois riverboat casinos, call the following toll-free numbers: *Alton Belle* Riverboat, (800) 336-7568; *Casino Queen* (East St. Louis), (800) 777-0777;

Empress I and *II* (Joliet), (800) 345-6789; *Grand Victoria* Casino (Elgin), (847) 888-1000; Harrah's *Northern Star* and *Southern Star* (Joliet), (800) 427-7247; Hollywood Casino's *City of Lights I* and *II* (Aurora), (800) 888-7777; Jumer's Casino Rock Island, (800) 477-7747; *Par-a-Dice* (Peoria), (800) 332-5634; *Players Riverboat Casino* (Metropolis), (800) 935-7700. Or contact the Illinois Bureau of Tourism, (800) 223-0121.

Fall

32

Amish Sojourn

ARTHUR AND ARCOLA

"HEY, PAPA! THERE'S A HITCHING POST AT THAT HARDEE'S," yells my daughter Kate, as we tour downtown Arcola, Illinois's second-largest Amish settlement.

Dayne, her younger sister, also has eagle-eyes for all things Amish. "Look at all these buggies! It's like a cowboy movie."

Well, not quite. But like I always say, "Plain and simple, there is nothing fancy about the Amish."

Amish Customs

Amish homes are nondescript white frame houses with no electricity, often without pictures, photographs, or mirrors. Traditional dress dictates black collarless coats and wide-brimmed hats for men, and solid-color full-length dresses and black bonnets over white prayer caps for women.

Horses provide transportation for most Amish sects, their black buggies clomping down modern paved highways as well as little-traveled country roads in ritualistic fashion.

And by tradition, most work the land, tilling their fields much as their 19th-century ancestors did—with horse and steel plow, muscle and sweat, on small 50- to 100-acre farms. (The Amish have a saying: "A horse reproduces, a tractor produces nothing but debts.")

Amish History

So the Amish continue today, living much as they did when they first arrived in America in 1728 from Switzerland, in search of religious freedom. The first group of Amish set up a colony of believers in Pennsylvania Dutch country. In their quest for rich soil, they came to the Midwest, with settlements taking hold across the heartland—the largest in Ohio and Indiana.

Today about 112 Amish settlements are scattered over North and South America. (Curiously enough, there are no longer any Amish in Europe, their place of origin.)

It's also interesting to note that more than 70 percent of present Amish settlements were established after 1940. And that despite living by the precepts of an 18th-century "Ordnung," a set of religious rules that govern every detail of their lives—including the clothes they wear, the food they eat, how they socialize, and even whether to use buttons or hooks to fasten shirts and trousers—their simple, unhurried lives continue much the same as the 21st century approaches.

Amish-Country Manners

To be good visitors when touring Amish settlements, remember that these people aren't acting out roles in re-created living-history villages. And that despite living in the midst of the "English" (non-Amish), they prize their privacy.

Also, many Amish sects prohibit members to be photographed. So don't be offended if your vacation snapshot is spoiled (especially by adults) by a timely pull of the hat or turn of the back. Or if a wave of the hand isn't returned (although it usually is). The real joy is found in watching these plain people continue in their centuries-old ways and customs.

Illinois Amish—Arthur

In Illinois, you can take a memorable trip back in time by visiting the state's largest Amish settlement in and around Arthur, located about 175 miles south of Chicago. Settled in the 1860s, it has been called "one of the most typical Amish towns."

About 300 Amish families are scattered over tidy farmsteads, all practicing their "plain ways." Black buggies clip-clop down dusty country roads while powerful Percheron, Belgian, and Clydesdale draft horses pull farm plows and other turn-of-the-century harvesting contraptions.

Intimate snapshots of everyday Amish life are best discovered by driving the back roads of this tiny farming community. You might see a young father showing his son how to drive a buggy, a team of four or more horses pulling a discing machine through farm fields, Amish kids on no-frills bicycles, or a typical Amish clothes dryer—rows of long dresses and black pants flapping in the wind on clotheslines.

About a hundred Amish country businesses are dotted around the rural landscape. (Pick up free maps for self-guided tours of out-of-the-way shops at the Amish Country Information Center on East Progress Street in Arthur. And remember that in most Amish communities, stores and even restaurants are closed on Sundays.) Most sought after are Amish quilts, whose expert handiwork fetches fancy prices;

figure on spending upward of $650 for a top-quality, queen-size handstitched quilt.

Other Amish shops offer handmade oak furniture (try F & B Woodworking), homemade candy (Arndt's Fudgery is a favorite), hickory-smoked bacon and hams (Das Schlacht Haus), and delicious homemade pies (Yoder's Country Kitchen in nearby Chesterville).

And note that some good Amish shops aren't on the Amish country tour map. So keep your eyes open for hand-lettered "business" signs near driveways and along country lanes.

Arcola

About nine miles east of Arthur sits Arcola, the state's other large Amish settlement. While it also has its share of Amish farm markets, bakeries, and restaurants (craft and antique shops inhabit restored brick buildings in its historic Main Street district), it is probably most well known for Rockome Gardens, a 200-acre park established by the late Elvan Yoder to share his Amish heritage.

Yoder constructed scores of rock-art sculptures and rock-featured colorful flower beds in the gardens—even the birdhouses are made from stone. Especially noteworthy is a folk-art castle made of broken 7-Up bottles. You also can tour herb gardens, vegetable gardens, and just about every other kind of garden imaginable.

Besides these beautiful natural settings, you also can visit the gardens' Amish home (furnished in the style of area Amish houses), an Amish one-room schoolhouse, a farm implement museum, and more.

If you'd rather ride than walk, hop aboard a train for a chug around the gardens. Or climb inside a horse-drawn Amish buggy and clip-clop 'round town.

Visit in August for Amish Farm Market Days, which feature an auction of 75 new Amish quilts. Or come during the mid-September/early October Harvest Festival, for horse-powered threshing demonstrations, plowing contests, silage cutting, and corn shucking.

A weekend trip to Amish country isn't complete without sampling some of the region's stick-to-your-ribs food. Rockome Gardens' Family Style Restaurant puts on a pretty good Illinois Amish (Dutch-style) buffet, complete with broasted chicken, Dutch sausage, veggies, noodles with creamy gravy, corn bread and beans, freshly baked cinnamon rolls slathered with locally produced apple butter, and more.

Of course, the best way to experience the Amish country is by spending some time with an Amish family. In fact, you can share a meal with local Amish in their home; arrangements are made through the Arthur Visitors Center.

For More Information

For more information about Rockome Gardens, call (217) 268-4106. For more Illinois Amish country information, contact the Arthur Information Center, 106 East Progress, Arthur, IL 61911, (800) 722-6474; or the Arcola Information Center, Box 274, Arcola, IL 61910, (217) 268-4530.

Amish Sojourn

33

The Great River Road

ALONG THE MISSISSIPPI RIVER

KNOW WHERE YOU CAN FIND THE ONLY PREHISTORIC NATIVE American city north of Mexico? How about the oldest French Colonial architecture in the Upper Midwest?

And what part of Illinois lies WEST of the Mississippi River?

The answers to these questions, and other believe-it-or-don't travel facts, can be found only by taking a ramble on the Illinois portion of the Great River Road.

It would take more than a month of weekends to explore the nooks and crannies of the GRR, a nationally designated pathway of blue highways, country roads, and village streets that cling to a scenic route flanking the Mississippi River as it twists, turns, and tumbles through Illinois.

But take your time. There's more than 500 miles of Great River Road from East Dubuque in northwestern Illinois to its southern Illinois terminus in Cairo. It's hard to get lost—the road is marked by distinctive white-and-green riverboat wheelhouse signs. And while there's plenty to enjoy along the way, there are some "shouldn't miss" highlights.

So here's a list of my top stops on the GRR, in no particular order.

Galena

Galena is probably the most well-known stop on the Illinois portion of the GRR. A historic lead-mining boomtown, Galena has the distinction of having about 85 percent of its Victorian mansions and turn-of-the-century commercial buildings listed on the National Register of Historic Places.

The town delights shoppers with more than 150 specialty shops, from fine arts galleries and fancy boutiques to antique stores and T-shirt shops. It's also the Midwest's bed-and-breakfast capital, with more than 40 inns scattered around town.

Among my favorites are the Aldrich Guest House, located across the Galena River but within walking distance of downtown; the Hellman Guest House, situated atop a bluff (Horseshoe Mound) with panoramic views of the church-steepled townscape; and the Pine Hollow Inn, less than two miles from Main Street yet a tranquil outpost situated on a 110-acre Christmas tree farm. Its hiking trails skirt up river bluffs, and sounds of howling coyotes fill the night.

Fall

Nauvoo

Situated near a bend of the Mississippi River in western Illinois, Nauvoo is a treasure trove of pioneer architecture, landmark buildings, and historical significance.

Multimillion-dollar restoration projects continue to unearth and reshape the area into a living-history monument to 19th-century pioneer America. Most tours are free at the dozens of historic riverfront homes, buildings, and commercial establishments that preserve this cultural wonderland, sometimes called the Williamsburg of the Midwest.

Founded in 1839 by Joseph Smith, spiritual leader of the Mormon Church, the city grew from a swampy trading post to a vibrant community of 11,000 with several handsome public buildings, fine residences, a printing plant that produced a citywide newspaper, and many trade and craft shops.

Prosperity could not prevent persecution by local non-Mormons, which culminated in the murder of Smith in nearby Carthage. Without his leadership, a schism developed within the religious community. Eventually most of Nauvoo's Mormons packed up their things in horse-drawn and human-pulled wagons and trekked westward under the leadership of Brigham Young to establish their permanent settlement in Utah.

Carthage

This Mormon historic site is a tragic one. A side trip to Carthage, 12 miles south of Nauvoo on State 96, then 14 miles east on U.S. Route 136, brings you to the Old Carthage Jail. Here, an enraged mob murdered Joseph Smith and his brother in 1844. The jail offers 30-minute guided tours, a 10-minute slide presentation, and exhibits.

Elsah/Alton/Grafton

Several southern Illinois Mississippi riverside communities are making a remarkable comeback from the destructive spring and summer floods of several years ago. A case in point is Elsah, whose clean-up effort has been heroic. The battering it took from raging floodwaters was tragic, especially when you consider that it was the first entire town ever to be placed on the National Register of Historic Places.

However, many of the historic 19th-century stone cottages and frame homes have been repaired to their former elegance. Consider overnighting at the Maple Leaf Cottage or Green Tree Inn, two splendid bed and breakfasts.

Alton is a great spot for winter eagle watching, especially among the limestone bluffs and woodlands that stretch along the confluence of the Mississippi and Illinois Rivers. Or take a cruise on the *Alton Belle Riverboat*, with unlimited-stakes casino gambling.

Grafton, huddled on the banks of the Illinois River, is proud of Pere Marquette State Park; at 8,000 acres, it's Illinois's largest. Check out the park's fabulous lodge, featuring luxury guest suites, whose elegance may not be equaled at any other Midwest state park lodge. Or if you'd rather get closer to nature, rent a room in one of seven natural-stone guest houses clinging to the Illinois River shoreline.

Fall

Collinsville

The only prehistoric Native American city north of Mexico awaits you at Cahokia Mounds State Historic Site in Collinsville. Not only can you walk among the preserved remains of the ancient city (try climbing the steps of the hand-built Monks Mound, a massive 100-foot-tall earthen platform), but the site's incredible interpretative center offers life-size dioramas, artifacts, and explanations of the social, political, and religious structures that governed this city (which at its zenith claimed nearly 20,000 people).

One mystery does elude archaeologists, however—its people disappeared without a trace almost 10,000 years ago.

Cahokia

It's not surprising that with all the French explorers plying the Mississippi during the 1700s some would eventually settle down and build homes. You can view some of the best examples of French Colonial architecture in Cahokia.

Most impressive are the 1799 Holy Family Church, a unique vertical timber structure; the 1740 Cahokia Courthouse, then the territory's governmental seat; and the Jarrot Mansion, a Federal-style brick home built in 1810 for French businessman Nicholas Jarrot.

Ellis Grove

Located about 60 miles south of Cahokia, this little town offers more slices of early Illinois history. The oldest site is Fort Kaskaskia, constructed years before the American Revolution to protect townspeople against British invaders. During the war, local militia burned the fortress to keep it out of British hands. Today, you can still see the earthworks around the fort's original perimeter.

The 1802 Pierre Menard Home has been called the "finest example of southern French Colonial architecture in this section of the Mississippi Valley." Tour this handsome white mansion, which was built for Illinois's first lieutenant governor.

And did you know that part of Illinois actually rests on the WEST side of the Mississippi? Kaskaskia Island is a sliver of land that not only stakes that claim, but is graced with the "Liberty Bell of the West." That's the bell, according to local lore, given by the French king to the community in 1743.

Legend says that the bell last rang out on July 4, 1778—to celebrate the defeat of the British by George Rogers Clark and his rangers, an action that "freed" the town.

FOR MORE INFORMATION

For more information about the above attractions, other stops along the Great River Road, and guidebooks/maps of the region, contact:

The Great River Road

Illinois Bureau of Tourism, (800) 223-0121

Galena/Jo Daviess County Convention and Visitors Bureau, (800) 747-9377

Aldrich Guest House, (815) 777-3323

Hellman Guest House, (815) 777-3638

Pine Hollow Inn, (815) 777-1071

Nauvoo Visitors Center, (217) 453-2237

Old Carthage Jail and Visitors Center, (217) 357-2989

Historic Elsah, (800) 258-6645 or (618) 465-6676

Maple Leaf Cottage Inn, (618) 374-1684

164

Green Tree Inn, (618) 374-2821

Alton Belle Riverboat Casino, (800) 336-7568

Pere Marquette State Park, (618) 786-2331

Cahokia Mounds State Historic Site, (618) 346-5160

Cahokia Courthouse State Historic Site (and Visitors Center), (618) 332-1782

Fort Kaskaskia and Kaskaskia Bell State Historic Sites, (618) 859-3741

Pierre Menard Home State Historic Site, (618) 859-3031

34

Up and Down on the Farm

HOW'D YOU'D LIKE TO TICKLE A COW BEHIND THE EARS? Watch a mama hen scuttle to fetch her youngins? Sniff some fresh-cut hay?

Or kiss a llama named Fernando?

Fernando Llama, get it?

The real question is "How you gonna keep 'em up in the city once they've been down on the farm?" If you'd like to try and answer that one, here are two of my favorite Illinois farm getaways that your family might enjoy.

Ya all come back now, ya hear?

Sweet Basil Hill Farm Though it's nestled on a hilltop about an hour's drive north of Chicago in Gurnee, just about halfway between the Windy City and Milwaukee, Sweet Basil Hill Farm is miles away from big-city pressures and problems. Even stress-dodging corporate executives from as far away as Osaka, Japan, have described this seven-and-a-half-acre country retreat as a "peaceful break from the doldrums of the real world."

Run by Bob and Terri Jones, the inn rests on a wooded hillside overlooking farm fields and miles of wild prairie. Sheep and two llamas (Fernando and Dalai) graze the back acres, always ready to rub noses with willing partners. Wild blackberry bushes abound, and hiking paths trace the farm's perimeter.

In winter, Bob grooms those trails for cross-country skiers, who can schuss into the woods and discover absolute tranquillity. Taking nature walks and chasing roosters and rabbits are other low-key pastimes.

Less ambitious guests may snuggle up in front of the inn's common room fireplace with a good book, try their hand at the spinning wheel, or hone their skills in the art of laziness.

Yep, it's the simple pleasures that count around these parts. Here's what happened on our first family visit here.

"You're the most colorful guests that have visited my sheep in more than two years," Bob said to Kate and Dayne as they headed to the barn in their neon-colored ski jackets for a visit with his 40-head flock.

That's why Sweet Basil Hill Farm remains one of my girls' favorite getaways—where else can they fuss over lovable barnyard creatures so close to our Chicago home?

Terri, a photographer, herb lover, and wool spinner, greeted us (as she does all guests) at the door. Step inside and you're in a world of handsome English and American country antiques, gleaming wood floors, eight-foot-tall cupboards and armoires, wicker rockers, and Shaker chairs.

My wife, Debbie, loved our second-floor, two-room suite filled with Laura Ashley linens, European feather comforters, and antique knickknacks. Kate found a crystal ball and told our fortunes before we could unpack the suitcases.

The downstairs Basil Room is another favorite with its Shaker-style pencil-post canopy bed and Amish quilt.

Breakfast in the knotty pine dining room is like dining inside a North Woods cabin. Seated at a long harvest table, we feasted on chicken, cheese and broccoli pastry puffs, cinnamon and cranberry rolls, fresh juices, and warm apple-cinnamon dumplings for dessert. Then we hiked the back acres to visit with sheep, chickens, and llamas.

Those llamas love to rub noses with guests. Kate didn't hesitate going schnoz-to-schnoz with Fernando. Dayne waited until she saw that Kate didn't lose anything in the bargain.

Bob, a successful professional actor, revels in giving tours of the place. That includes hikes to the inn's "hugging tree."

Says Bob, "Hug it and you'll have 7 years' good luck. Feel silly about it, and you get 11 years."

Also get Bob to tell you some of the sheep's names, especially the story of how Johann Sebastian Baa and Half Jack got their monikers.

Hobson's Bluffdale   Hobson's Bluffdale is a 320-acre farm (soybeans, corn, wheat, and a few pigs) in Eldred (located in southwest Illinois) run by Libby and Bill Hobson; it's been in Bill's family since 1828 and was named by his great-great-grandfather for bluffs that run through the property.

On my last visit here, Libby took me into the original stone farmhouse. It's the cooking headquarters, and also contains some of Bill's priceless family heirlooms, including a four-volume family history written by his great-great-grandfather.

"Charles Dickens was one of his friends," Bill told me, "and visited here in the 1840s. They had to pick up Dickens at the train in a spring wagon and bring him to the farm."

Bluffdale is a spectacular getaway for anyone—but especially for city slickers and kids. Bill and Libby encourage everyone to help with regular farm chores—feeding the chickens and pigs, gathering eggs, moving geese, bottle-feeding calves, picking fresh blackberries, harvesting vegetables from Bill's two-acre garden, and more.

Libby is the cook who takes all this delicious farm-fresh food and whips up great feasts. Family-style meals include eggs, French toast or pancakes, fruits, and home-baked breads for breakfast; maybe a picnic lunch packed for a trek through the woods; and supper table specials like fried chicken, baked ham, pot roast, barbecued pork chops—

Up and Down on the Farm

topped off with oven-fresh sweets and homemade ice cream.

"I'm a city girl," Libby said. "Never set foot on a farm until I met Bill when we were both students at the University of Illinois." Bill steps right in with a zinger. "That's right. She saw giraffes and zebras at the city zoo long before she ever saw any of my farm animals."

Guests can relax under a 300-year-old burr oak tree or walk to the outdoor rec hall for a game of pool. Maybe you just want to settle in an old-fashioned rocker on the porch; that's OK, too.

Overnight rooms are spartan, but comfortable, done in bandana reds and blues. You don't come to Bluffdale for roomside splendor; there's far too much to do. The flexible schedule includes archaeological digs (this is historic Indian country), Saturday night square dances, Sunday ice cream socials, Monday ball games, Friday night bonfire sing-alongs, and Tuesday afternoon cookout picnics at Greenfield Lake.

For More Information

For room rates and other information, contact the Sweet Basil Hill Farm, 15397 West Washington Street, Gurnee, IL 60031; (800) 228-HERB or (847) 244-3333. The farm has three rooms, including two suites, all with private bath and air-conditioning. It's open year-round.

Hobson's Bluffdale, Hillview Road, Eldred, IL 62027; (217) 983-2854. It has eight rooms, with three two-room suites, all with private bath and air-conditioning. It's open all year as a bed and breakfast; weekly farm vacation sessions are available March through November.

35

Ghastly Gourds

SYCAMORE

GHOSTS, GHOULIES, AND GOBLINS MAKE GREAT GOOSEBUMPS. But now you can add ghastly gourds to your Halloween hijinks list.

See for yourself when thousands of prize-winning carved pumpkins are displayed on the DeKalb County Courthouse lawn during Sycamore's annual Pumpkin Festival, a late-October Midwest mainstay and one of the region's largest gourd soirees.

This long-running, four-day celebration of "everything pumpkin" has transformed this sleepy farming community into the self-declared "Decorated Pumpkin Capital of the World." You'll see happy, garrulous, gap-toothed pumpkin faces mixed with sinister-looking jack-o'-lanterns—and, shades of Jurassic Park, you might even see a frightening, seven-foot-tall tyrannosaur made completely out of pumpkin shells.

In recent years, "celebrity look-alike" carved pumpkins have become a popular attraction. Sycamore gourd classics already have included likenesses of Snoopy (of *Peanuts* and "Great Pumpkin" fame); E.T., whose head somewhat resembled a squashed pumpkin; Garfield, the bumptious feline with the bright orange coat who looks as if he might have swallowed a pumpkin whole; and even Presidents Ronald Reagan and Bill Clinton.

Another festival highlight is the Pumpkin Parade, featuring festive marching bands, floats, and specialty units—all celebrating Sycamore's pumpkin legacy. The parade winds along the quaint tree-lined streets of the city's historic district, usually on Sunday afternoon. The best spots for setting up lawn chairs or claiming curb space for viewing the parade are along Somonauk, State, and Locust Streets.

Later you can browse through the Pumpkin Festival Flea Market and Antique Show at Sycamore High School, where merchandise booths and aisles are stuffed with handmade crafts, valuable antiques, and collectibles. Free buses take visitors from the downtown area to this event.

Or head to the pumpkin baked goods contest, an art fair in the courthouse lobby, and a pumpkin pie-eating contest held on the Courthouse lawn. This is a "can't-miss" competition for spectators, especially since contestants cannot use their hands to eat the pies. Count on lots of orange faces by the time a winner is declared.

Of course, you won't be shortchanged on scares and terrors. A Halloween Haunted House is set up (usually on Main Street) across from the courthouse. Rattling chains, creepy crawlers, and other kinds of fiendish scare tactics should provide thrills and chills for any soul brave enough to enter the possessed manse.

And throughout the festival, tasty food, snacks, and all kinds of pumpkin treats can be purchased at food stands operated by local not-for-profit community organizations.

For More Information

For more Pumpkin Festival information, call (815) 895-5161; or contact the Greater Sycamore Chamber of Commerce, (815) 895-3456.

36

Shawnee Ramble

SOUTHERN ILLINOIS

MENTION SOUTHERN ILLINOIS AND PEOPLE USUALLY ENVISION endless rows of cornstalks swaying in a gentle breeze. Or lazy rivers meandering through flat pastureland dotted only by slow-moving cows looking for a shady spot under a tree.

Yet a ride over the region's back roads reveals a much different landscape: tall limestone bluffs overlook the Mississippi and Ohio Rivers, which separate the southern portion of the state from Missouri and Kentucky; fantastic rock formations and lush flora abound throughout the Shawnee National Forest, an extension of the Missouri Ozarks; and a seemingly endless supply of tree-bordered lakes provides perfect spots for all kinds of "fish and swim" adventures.

Besides all the natural wonders, southern Illinois is home to several fascinating remnants of the past. Just east of St. Louis rise the enigmatic Cahokia Mounds, built by prehistoric Indians; gracious river towns are an antique hunter's delight; and an impressive fort crowns high bluffs, a reminder of the state's pre–Revolutionary War days.

It's perfect territory for weekend wanderings. Of course, if you have more time to explore the region, don't limit yourself to the suggestions described below; a journey down one of the region's inviting country roads is likely to end at yet another charming river town, pristine lake, or shady hiking trail.

Day One

This southern Illinois ramble begins at the Cahokia Mounds (see Chapter 21 for a more detailed description of this historic site). Built by members of the Mississippian culture around A.D. 900, this extraordinary group of more than 60 mounds was an urban center with a population of about 20,000.

Conical mounds were used as burial grounds; the more numerous rectangular ones, with sloping sides and flat tops, supported huge wooden buildings inhabited by the village's elite. These earthworks were built up using basketfull after basketfull of earth—a remarkable feat considering their size. Monks Mound, the largest flat-topped mound north of Mexico, covers 14 acres and rises in four terraces to a height of more than a hundred feet. Another eye-catcher is Woodhenge, a reconstructed calendar circle of wooden posts.

The Cahokia Mounds Museum Society sponsors ongoing digs at the site. Volunteers are welcome, but you must sign up in advance to take part in the archaeological activities. Many of the artifacts unearthed in excavations are displayed in the site's first-rate museum, which also explains the construction of the mounds and the civilization that lived here before disappearing without a trace.

The annual "Rediscover Cahokia Days" (usually held in August) celebrate the cultures of more recent Native Americans with dances, special exhibits, and demonstrations of arrowhead making and other traditional crafts. For museum and other information, call (618) 346-5160.

The next stop is Fort de Chartes State Historic Site, located near Prairie du Rocher, about 50 miles southwest of the mounds. A much different kind of monument to past cultures, this stone fort was built at enormous cost by the French in 1753. It served as the seat of government for their colony in the New World, which once occupied the entire Mississippi Valley; it also provided protection for the lucrative fur trade. And during the French and Indian War, it was an important center for military operations.

In 1765, the fort was ceded to victorious British troops. Today, the guardhouse, gatehouse, and the fort's massive stone north wall (itself enough to inspire awe) have been reconstructed. The powder magazine, however, is the original—making it one of the oldest buildings in Illinois.

Traditional 18th-century crafts are often demonstrated on summer weekends, and artifacts found on the site are displayed at the Peithman Museum. (Due to occasional flooding, the site sometimes does not open until late summer or early fall.) Call (618) 284-7230.

The last leg of the day's journey is a drive to Carbondale, a boisterous college town. Along the way, you can enjoy fabulous vistas of the Mississippi River. Or stop in Ellis Grove, where you can tour the 1802 French Colonial Pierre Menard Home State Historic Site, the mansion of Illinois's first lieutenant governor; call (618) 859-3031.

Another Ellis Grove option is a visit to Fort Kaskaskia, built several years before the American Revolution to protect the region from British attack. Later, townspeople burned it to the ground to prevent English troops from capturing it, so all that remains today are the earthworks around the fort's perimeter. Call (618) 859-3741.

The Kaskaskia Bell, known as the "Liberty Bell of the West," is located on Kaskaskia Island, the only part of Illinois on the west side of the Mississippi River. The bell rang on July 4, 1778, to celebrate the village's liberation from the British by George Rogers Clark and his rangers; call (618) 859-3741 for directions.

And just past Grimsby, the road is lined with the tall trees of the Shawnee National Forest.

When you get to Carbondale, head for Crab Orchard Lake, a 7,000-acre splash noted for great camping, picnick-

Shawnee Ramble

ing, and water fun. If you prefer to sleep behind four walls, drive on to Giant City State Park, just east of Makanda. Its impressive stone-and-log Giant City Lodge was built in the 1930s by the Civilian Conservation Corps. Adjacent to the lodge are log cabins, each with a terrific view of the forest's rolling hills. Hearty dinners are served in the lodge's rustic dining room.

Be sure to reserve plenty of time for exploration of the 3,700-acre park itself. Paths leading from the lodge pass monolithic rock formations, streaked with shades of red ranging from maroon to apricot, and more than 70 varieties of trees—including dogwood, wild apple, and oak (of which there are 40 species alone). Along Red Cedar Trail, a 16-mile loop (there's a campsite midway), you'll discover pockets of prairie grass, coal outcroppings, black oaks, and huge pine trees. Call (618) 457-4836 (park), or (618) 457-4921 (lodge).

Day Two

Leaving Giant City, head east across the state to Golconda, Illinois's first planned community, located on the banks of the Ohio River. This sleepy town is home to the Mansion of Golconda, an 1895 red-brick Victorian complete with original stained-glass windows, six fireplaces, fine woodwork, and other architectural gems.

It offers guest rooms for overnighters, but it gains much of its reputation for a dining room serving up delicious meals of everything from sautéed chicken livers, honey-crisp chicken, and fried steaks to catfish Camille (a spicy, grilled taste of heaven) and shrimp stuffed with cold crabmeat. The food is so good that several Illinois governors, including Jim Edgar, made the mansion a regular meal stop during their journeys around the state. Call (618) 683-4400.

The mansion is a good base for excursions into the 263,000-acre Shawnee National Forest, filled with vistas of ever-changing foliage framing massive rock formations and anomalies of nature created during the Ice Age. Many of the forest's highlights are scattered along a circular route that eventually leads back to Golconda.

Your first stop is Cave-in-Rock. After gazing at the Ohio River from the top of the cave's smooth limestone cowl, take a hike through the 40-foot-wide, 25-foot-high cave below, which burrows far back into the bluff. Once a landmark for keelboat captains ferrying settlers over the river to points west, Cave-in-Rock served as a lair for the infamous Samuel Mason. A former Revolutionary War colonel, the nefarious Mason presided over a ragtag gang of escaped felons, robbers, and New Orleans harlots.

Innocent river passengers were lured into the cave by the inscription "Liquor Vault and House of Entertainment," etched by Mason over the cave's mouth. Once inside the cave, they were robbed—or worse. After Mason fled under pressure from the law, other pirate gangs took his place; years later, they were finally chased out for good by local vigilantes. Today only hikers and other sightseers lurk within the cave's shadowy recesses.

Overnighters might like to stay in one of four duplex cabins located in Cave-in-Rock State Park; the eight suites each have great vistas of the Ohio River. Call (618) 289-4325.

Next up is Pounds Hollow Lake, where you can cool off in refreshing waters and sunbathe on a pleasant beach. You'll need a break, because next you'll hike the Rim Rock Forest Trail, which winds past some of the state's most startling geological wonders. You'll encounter enormous boulders, which the earth coughed up in a number of pre-glacial faults, and bizarre limestone and sandstone formations. Also, the stone remnants of an ancient Indian wall are scattered around the Pounds, a circular 50-acre tract sandwiched between rugged sandstone cliffs.

Shawnee Ramble

You can either hike (via the Rim Rock Trail) or drive to the Garden of the Gods, perhaps the most unusual spot in the Shawnee. Flagstone paths weave through 200-million-year-old rocks eroded into spectacular shapes, which bear names like Camel Rock, Fat Man's Squeeze, Tower of Babel, and Woman's Cave. An interpretative display near the parking lot explains the rocks' formation.

On the way back to Golconda, stop at Indian Kitchen, a tall rock shelf with a panoramic view of Lusk Creek Canyon. Here you'll discover some of Illinois's most rugged terrain. Only experienced hikers should attempt to climb the narrow trail up to the top of the precipice. However, anyone will feel comfortable on the path leading from the hamlet of Eddyville into the canyon itself, which is walled in by 100-foot-high cliffs.

Nearby is Bell Smith Springs, a mass of sheer cliffs, hulking boulders, and winding canyons pocked with caves where ancient Indians once resided. Downstream from the springs is a natural stone bridge, an immense rock arch curving to a height of 30 feet. While resting here, listening to the trilling of songbirds, you half expect Daniel Boone to come tramping out of the forest.

For More Information

For more information about Shawnee National Forest, contact the Shawnee National Forest, (618) 253-7114, or the Illinois Bureau of Tourism, (800) 223-0121.

Fall

37

Canal Capers

LEMONT TO LA SALLE

IT'S BEEN CALLED "A DERELICT DITCH SIX FEET DEEP" THAT straggles 97 miles westward from the pillars of Chicago's Stevenson Expressway until reaching its terminus near La Salle and Peru. But it's the canal that built Chicago's "big shoulders" and was proclaimed the centerpiece of America's first National Heritage Corridor, signed into law by President Ronald Reagan in 1984.

In effect, it became our first "national linear park," a zigzag of historic navigational channels, with some stretches still filled by stagnant waters.

I'm describing the Illinois & Michigan Canal, a shallow waterway opened in April 1848 to allow continuous commercial boat traffic between the Mississippi River, the Great Lakes, the Gulf of Mexico, and the eastern seaboard. It allowed Chicago to develop into a vital hub in transcontinental business and commerce.

Another legacy: built at a cost of $6.5 million, the I & M Canal became one of our nation's first massive public works programs. And it remained important to Chicago's growing commercial reputation until the railroads came along in the late 19th century and rendered canal transportation obsolete.

Today's tourists can't float a boat down the canal like travelers of the past. But they can retrace the canal's towpath by car, hiking, biking—even skiing. In fact, there are 41 communities along the canal that boast everything from historic buildings (maintained by the National Park Service) to museums explaining canal history.

Here's how the Park Service's own brochure sets the mood for a visit along the I & M National Heritage Corridor:

"If inhabitants of today's noisy world of truck exhausts, roaring railroads and jet engines were by some magic to watch the I & M Canal covered with boats, they would be astonished at the quiet.

"The only sounds to be heard would be the movements of mules along the towpaths and the conversations of the boatmen."

If only that quiet could return to our world.

While you'll probably start an I & M Canal tour in Romeoville or Lockport, note that the canal originally stretched all the way into Chicago. In fact, the Bridgeport neighborhood (famous for breeding Chicago mayors, like the Daleys) was the site of canal groundbreaking ceremonies in July 1836. If you drive south on Lake Shore Drive, go to I-55 and continue to Harlem Avenue, you might be surprised to learn that you've been driving along what once was a good portion of the I & M Canal (which made way for this very highway).

Why a canal here? Actually, this area already was used by Native Americans, who portaged their canoes between the Des Plaines and Chicago Rivers; so it was an obvious spot to link up two existing waterways and "bring them" to Chicago.

In fact, the Chicago Portage National Historic Site is located near here, commemorating the site where Father Marquette and Louis Jolliet came ashore in 1673 as the first Europeans to explore the area.

In Lemont, the I & M Canal appears not much different than it did in 1848, mainly because it was totally constructed (sides and bottom) of limestone bedrock, which had to be cut through as a final step in building the canal. Just a few miles down the canal route is Romeoville, which boasts the Isle la Cache Museum located on an 80-acre island; it offers both displays and living-history programs showcasing the canal, as well as the historic French and Indian fur trade.

Lockport, just five miles to the south, is where the first of 15 locks on the canal was built. It's also the heart of today's historic I & M Heritage Corridor. Among the town's 37 historic sites, highlights include the Will County Historical Society Canal Museum, originally the headquarters of the canal commissioners; the Gaylord Building, the oldest structure along the I & M, made of golden yellow native limestone and containing a National Park Service visitor center; and Lock 1, which was used to raise and lower boats on the canal system. Come here during Lockport's annual Old Canal Days, celebrated in June, for even more towpath history.

Continuing south, Channahon State Park accesses the I & M Canal State Trail, a 15-mile paved-over section of the canal that's now a favorite of hikers, bikers, and (in the winter) cross-country skiers. Twenty miles farther southwest, in Morris, you'll find Locks 6 and 7. Number 6 directs water into the Des Plaines River; you also can tour a restored lockkeeper's house. Number 7 spills water back into the canal channel.

Morris's Gebhard Woods once held the tallest tree in Illinois. But in 1992, high winds toppled the 120-foot-tall eastern cottonwood, which had measured 32 feet around.

Also near Morris, an access hiking trail leads to Lock 8, where you can tour a restored locktender's house and see an aqueduct that carried the I & M Canal over Aux Sable Creek. And just outside Morris is Goose Lake Prairie State Natural Area, the largest remnant of virgin tallgrass prairie in Illinois. Take time to stroll its hiking paths, crisscrossing the park's 2,500 acres; grasses here grow higher than a horse's shoulder, reaching up to 12 feet. It's one of the few

Canal Capers

places in the Land of Lincoln where you get a historically accurate portrayal of what Illinois really looked like more than 150 years ago, before sod-busting settlers tamed this ocean of grasses.

The National Park Service heralds the Seneca Grain Elevator, located in that little namesake canal-route ghost town. Built in 1861–62, the 65-foot-tall, 70,000-bushel elevator is similar to scores of like structures that lined the I & M during the 19th century.

In Ottawa, 14 miles west of Seneca, you'll see the largest of four aqueducts that carried the I & M over four other waterways. Another Ottawa claim to fame—it was the site of the first Lincoln–Douglas debate in 1858. Records show that nearly 10,000 people showed up to hear the fireworks, which took place in Washington Park, still the town square.

You're almost at the end of your tour upon reaching Utica, about 25 miles farther west along the canal towpath. The La Salle County Historical Society Museum, on the bank of the I & M Canal, itself is quite interesting, located in a restored pre–Civil War stone warehouse. Be sure to visit Starved Rock State Park, too; its natural beauty includes 18 canyons, deep gorges, waterfalls, and majestic sandstone bluffs.

And sneak a peek at the park's stone-and-timber lodge, constructed by the Civilian Conservation Corps in 1933. It's a great place to headquarter your family while exploring the I & M Canal corridor. At least take a look at its Great Hall, decorated with Native American artifacts and featuring a massive stone fireplace.

At the western end of the canal is La Salle-Peru. Here is where cargoes were transferred from canal traffic to steamboats for the voyage down the Illinois River, along the Mississippi, and even to the Gulf of Mexico.

It's your last chance to take a glimpse of the past. Lock 14 has been restored to look much like all 15 locks appeared in their 1850s canal-traffic heydays. And farther down a hiking trail is the restored Vermilion Aqueduct.

For More Information

For a brochure describing I & M touring highlights, call the Illinois Bureau of Tourism, (800) 223-0121; or contact the Illinois & Michigan Canal Visitors Center in Lockport, (815) 838-4830. For details about overnighting at the Starved Rock State Park Lodge, call (815) 667-4211.

Canal Capers

38

An Honest Abe Thanksgiving

PETERSBURG

BACK IN THE MID-1800S, THERE WAS NO SUCH THING AS "Thanksgiving Day." Occasionally presidents would declare a "day of thanksgiving" on a variety of dates—but these were set aside for prayer and fasting rather than celebration.

(In fact, Illinois's first official statewide Thanksgiving Day, proclaimed by Gov. Thomas Carlin, was held on December 29, 1842; he also urged citizens "to meet in their respective houses of worship" on the appointed day.)

But a future president did celebrate a Thanksgiving Day of sorts in the 1830s when his tiny hamlet of New Salem, located on the Sangamon River in St. Petersburg, about 20 miles northwest of Springfield, annually heralded the completion of another successful harvest.

Usually held in mid-November, these harvest feasts featured all kinds of merrymaking, including hearty meals, games, music, dancing, and probably a wrestling match or two outside the local tavern.

Now you can join in the late-autumn fun during the annual Harvest Feast at Lincoln's New Salem State Historic Site, a full weekend of activities held in mid-November.

Abe Lincoln lived here from 1831 to 1837, holding a variety of jobs in this log cabin village that features 12 re-created timber houses, the Rutledge Tavern, 10 workshops, stores, saw and grist mills, and a school. All have been erected on the buildings' original sites and furnished with authentic artifacts of the period—with many articles being those actually used by New Salem people of Lincoln's time.

During the Harvest Feast, costumed interpreters perform chores and prepare meals that would traditionally occur at this time of year.

You'll see pioneer women dyeing wool, dipping candles, and cooking hearty feasts in most of the log buildings. The blacksmith's clanging anvil will beat a tattoo throughout the town, while other craftspeople will be busy making soap, shoes, clothes, and brooms to prepare for the winter season.

There'll also be kids' games (hoop rolling, sack races, and more), dancing and shooting contests, and a grand military parade conducted by the New Salem Militia.

The militia plays an important role in the festivities. During the 1830s, all white male residents of Illinois between the ages of 18 and 45 had to join the local guard.

During the fest, the New Salem unit entertains by reenacting a fall muster with plenty of action each day.

There's a flag raising at the Carding Mill; infantry drills near Rutledge Tavern; black-powder shooting contests behind the Onstot Barn; another mustering drill near the mill; and a military parade through the village, ending at the flagpole.

Also make sure that you stroll through the village to get a better idea of how Abe and his neighbors lived in pioneer Illinois. Some highlights:

- The Henry Onstot Cooper Shop is the only original building left from New Salem. It was quite important, too, since all produce was shipped in barrels at that time; Onstot's prices ranged from 40 cents for a flour barrel to $1.00 for a pork barrel. A crude washtub was a luxury at $1.50.

- At the Rutledge Tavern, travelers could enjoy a full meal and a bed for 37.5 cents per day, with the rates set by law.

- The Denton Offut Store first employed Lincoln in 1831 to take merchandise by flatboat from Springfield to New Orleans; Abe returned here to run the store. Later he held various jobs in the village, including woodchopper, postmaster, and deputy surveyor.

He also was elected to the Illinois General Assembly in 1834 (after losing a race in 1832) while he resided in New Salem.

But don't bother searching the village for Abe's old house; he never owned a home here, just rented rooms from various families.

Lincoln's "harvest feast" days must have made a lasting impression on him. While president, he made several Thanksgiving Day proclamations; however, most of them coincided with Civil War military operations.

But in his final 1864 Thanksgiving Day order, Abe declared that the last Thursday in November be set aside as a day of celebration.

Finally, using Lincoln's formula, FDR declared Thanksgiving an annual national holiday in 1939.

FOR MORE INFORMATION

Admission to the Harvest Feast is free. Lincoln's New Salem State Historic Site is located two miles south of Petersburg on State 97. For more information, contact the site at RR 1, P.O. Box 244A, Petersburg, IL 62675; (217) 632-4000.

An Honest Abe Thanksgiving

39

An Oregon Outing

IF YOU'RE A DIE-HARD LEAF PEEPER, SET YOUR AUTUMN SIGHTS on a weekend ramble to Oregon—not the state, but the town nestled in the Rock River Valley, just 90 minutes west of Chicago.

Surrounded by three tree-studded state parks and forests, crammed with antique shops fronting cobbled streets, and boasting a handsome turn-of-the-century town square, Oregon is a place to set your own pace while buoyed by a healthy dose of Midwest friendliness.

October visitors can laze by the gently flowing Rock River while gazing at bluff tops blazing with autumn colors. You can wander through Conover Square, an old brick piano factory transformed into a shopper's mecca. Or go pet a deer at White Pines Deer Park and climb aboard the 102-foot-long paddlewheeler *Rose of the Rock River* for a cruise.

Outdoor lovers and color hounds shouldn't miss hikes through the surrounding nature preserves. Castle Rock State Park is renowned for breathtaking river-valley views from atop its sandstone bluffs. You even can rent a log cabin at White Pines Forest State Park.

Atop a 250-foot bluff in Lowden State Park stands the awesome Chief Black Hawk statue overlooking the Rock River. The 48-foot-tall sculpture of the Fox and Sauk chief, completed by Lorado Taft in 1911, remains Oregon's most famous landmark.

The privately owned 2,300-acre Sinissippi Forest is covered with Norway spruce, Fraser fir, and white pine that will be on the market in early winter as chop-your-own Christmas trees.

Vintage architecture abounds in Oregon. Ogle County Courthouse, a National Historic Site built in the 1890s, has undergone a $1.5 million face-lift. Many old homes are worthy of a drive-by tour, and one Oregon mansion has been transformed into an elegant bed and breakfast.

One of my personal favorites, Pinehill Bed and Breakfast Inn, is an 1874 villa built by one of the town's first wealthy merchants. It's graced with fine antiques and comfortable guest rooms, including one named for W. Somerset Maugham, the man of letters, who often visited Pinehill during the 1930s. Maugham perhaps warmed himself by the room's marble fireplace, but the sumptuous whirlpool tub is a modern-day luxury. (And aren't we lucky!)

Innkeeper Sharon Burdick serves English teas with pastries and chocolates in the setting of a crackling fireplace, candlelight, and classical music.

Despite these upper-crust niceties, Pinehill is also a comfortable family inn. In fact, on my last visit here, my two daughters sprawled out on the living room floor playing Monopoly while other guests enjoyed treats at the dining room table. Afterward, the kids took long runs on the mansion's sprawling green lawns. It remains one of our most appealing homes away from home.

Dinner theater is on the menu in the Pump Room at Gaston's White Pines Inn. A perennial favorite is *Scrooge*, ticketed for December.

White Pines Ranch, the only Midwest dude ranch just for kids, offers fall and winter activities that include horseback trots, hayrides, campfire sing-alongs, sledding, ice skating, and snowmobiling.

One of the best times to visit Oregon is during its late September/early October "Autumn on Parade" festival. This family-style affair features a penny carnival, country-style barbecue, milking derby, pig scramble, and pennies-in-the-straw hunts. And the fall colors are spectacular.

FOR MORE INFORMATION

For more information, contact the Oregon Chamber of Commerce, (815) 732-2100; or Pinehill Bed and Breakfast, 400 Mix Street, Oregon, IL 61061, (815) 732-2061.

An Oregon Outing

40

Stepping Back into Time

ELSAH

YOU CAN STEP BACK INTO THE STEAMBOAT ERA OF THE 19TH century in a little town at the foot of great limestone bluffs, only a stone's throw away from the Mississippi River, that appears much as it did in pre–Civil War days.

Elsah is far from being another Galena, where attempts to restore 19th-century charm have resulted in a sometimes maddening tourist haven. Rather, Elsah portrays a graphic picture of a more tranquilly paced life in a river town as it really was lived during the 1850s.

In fact, the entire village is listed on the National Register of Historic Places. Named in 1853 by Scotsman James Semple after Ailsa Craig, a huge rock in the Firth of Clyde that's the last bit of Scot homeland one saw when sailing to America, the hamlet stretches along only two main streets (Mill and LaSalle), and each is lined with fine examples of steamboat-era buildings. (You can buy walking-tour books at shops in town.)

The first building on LaSalle off River Road is the Riverview House, Elsah's oldest, which began as a log cabin in 1847; the "new" section was added just after the Civil War.

Some call the Onetto-Bradley House Elsah's finest. Built in the late 1850s, then renovated in 1882, it displays arched windows and a cupola that ooze charm and grace.

Walk on and you'll come to the 1879 Keller Store, whose ice cream parlor was called the "bon ton place to go" in the 1880s. It's now home to the Elsah Landing Bakery and Tea Room. Every town resident I met told me that an Elsah visit is not complete without sampling their scrumptious goodies. And they were correct.

But there's lots more to Elsah than historic buildings. The town is right on the 16-mile-long Vadalabene Bike Trail, running along the base of tall limestone bluffs; it leads into Grafton and breathtaking views of the confluence of the Mississippi and Illinois Rivers along the Great River Road.

Sailboat regattas often take place on the Mississippi, which is just a short stroll away; sometimes you can see the *Delta Queen* passing by.

The American bald eagle winters along the river near Elsah. Scores can be spotted daily soaring high above the riverbanks from December through March.

It's also fun to take the tiny Brussels River Ferry (free) across the river to Calhoun County's scenic rolling hills of apple and peach orchards. And Elsah is 15 minutes from more than 40 antique shops and some of the better bargains in the Midwest.

Overnighting is no problem. The Maple Leaf Cottage Inn, a historic 1890s building, has been restored into an exceptional country guest house. Innkeeper Patty Taetz's home-cooked dinners are also a treat; consider boneless breast of chicken baked in herbs and butter or flounder stuffed with crab, country green veggies, rice with pecans, specialty cheesecake, and more. Of course, a full gourmet breakfast also comes with the room. Call (618) 374-1684.

Another excellent choice is the Green Tree Inn, a re-created 1850 general mercantile. The first-floor store offers quality arts and crafts like Shaker boxes, New England glass, and imported lace. Second-floor guest rooms are decorated in Victorian, Federal, and Country styles.

The inn also hosts a series of workshops throughout the year that include cooking demonstrations, flower arranging, landscaping, and more. A gourmet-style continental breakfast is included with room prices, which are $69 to $105. Call (618) 374-2821.

And I recommend the Finn Inn, in nearby Grafton, for terrific down-home fish dinners. Its unique decor, large aquariums beside the dining booths, complements the meal choices of turtle soup, chowder, one-pound whole catfish, fried turtle, and delicious pies like chocolate meringue. The town also claims more than 20 antique shops.

FOR MORE INFORMATION

Elsah is located on the Great River Road (McAdams Highway) between Grafton and Alton, about 40 minutes northwest of St. Louis. For more information, call Historic Elsah, (800) 258-6645 or (618) 465-6676; or contact the Illinois Bureau of Tourism, (800) 223-0121.

Winter

41

Road to Utopia

BISHOP HILL

IT'S SUNRISE ON CHRISTMAS MORNING, AND HARDY VISITORS are bundled in winter coats as they worship in the black-walnut pews of the Colony Church in the historic settlement of Bishop Hill.

The 1848 building has no heat, but that doesn't seem to bother anyone. The Christmas congregation is huddled in a candlelit church to celebrate Julotta, a traditional Swedish holiday service that greets the day of Jesus' birth.

Every year, this inspiring nondenominational service, held on December 25, is spoken in both Swedish and English. For 45 minutes, visitors can experience how Christmas Day started for long-ago settlers of this landmark pioneer utopian community.

Colony Church was the first permanent building constructed in the village that was to become known as Bishop Hill, site of a communal-style settlement established in 1846 on this sweeping stretch of prairie. The Swedish immigrants (led by Eric Jansson) who came to America in search of religious freedom founded the town and their lives on a belief in simple living, hard work, and worship.

Religion occupied a central role in the lives of these settlers. In fact, they attended church services twice daily for three-hour sessions and three times on Sunday for three-hour sessions—that's a total of 45 hours of weekly worship!

That's one of the reasons Julotta feels so special at Bishop Hill. Besides worship and prayer, Christmas Day's early morning service also features classical music played on a historic pump organ—a difficult task for the musician, who may have to contend with frigid fingers. Christmas hymns also are sung during holiday worship.

Of course, the good folks at Bishop Hill wouldn't think of sending visitors away without a little extra Christmas cheer. After the service, hot coffee and rusks (toasted sweet breads) are served in the church museum, which also displays historic paintings of life in the colony. Note that the church is the only building among the site's 13 original structures that is open on Christmas Day.

More people visit Bishop Hill when the summer and fall sun provides more comfortable surroundings. Many are surprised to learn that historians have called the village "America's most successful communal religious utopia." By the 1850s, the colony was plowing more than 12,000 acres of virgin prairie soil and producing huge food crops; it erected more than 20 large commercial buildings; and it became a commercial center of sorts, located between Rock Island and Peoria.

Property and wealth were shared by all settlers in the community, which soon gained added prominence for its master craftsmanship. That handiwork can still be seen in the simply decorated church, with its handhewn pews and chandeliers crafted of wood and wrought iron.

With the death of Jansson in 1850, internal dissension beset the colony. By 1861, the community had dissolved its property and wealth, evenly dividing profits among the remaining settlers.

Today, the colony (a state historic site) retains much of the charm, ambience, and architecture of its earlier heritage.

Most of the remaining 13 original buildings are open to visitors; and descendants of the first colonists continue to live and work in the community, some speaking Swedish as fluently as English.

You'll love the unhurried atmosphere of the tours here. It gives you plenty of time to explore historic nooks and crannies of the village and its architecture.

The crown jewel of Bishop Hill remains the Colony Church. It's a two-story structure, with the sanctuary located on the second floor; note the center divider separating traditional men's and women's pews. Originally, the first floor and lower level (basement) were divided into 10 rooms each, where many of the first colonists made their homes. (Remember that the church was the first building constructed at Bishop Hill.) Now the lower level contains a museum displaying Swedish and early colony artifacts.

Be sure to visit the Steeple Building, a three-story Greek Revival structure, constructed of handmade bricks covered with plaster and completed in 1854. Perhaps its most unique feature is the two-story wooden steeple that contains a clock with four faces, but only one hand. Local folklore attributes this oddity to the colony's work ethic: "If you take care of the hours, you don't have to worry about the minutes."

A number of rooms are restored to their 19th-century appearance, and there's a collection of common articles used by settlers dating to the mid-1800s. Especially interesting is a half-hour color slide presentation documenting the history of Bishop Hill.

Also take a peek at the Colony Hotel (called Bjorklund locally). Built in 1852, the two-story brick building has undergone many changes from its original use as the village dormitory. It operated as a fine guest house until the 1920s. Today the first floor and a guest room have been restored to 1860s style.

Road to Utopia

If you'd like to "live" a little bit of Bishop Hill history, visit during one of its many annual festivals. August's "Sommar-marknad" is a summer market featuring fresh produce, home-baked goods, and pioneer crafts and demonstrations. "Jordbruksdagarna," in late September, is the colony's agricultural days; you'll find horse-drawn plow teams harvesting broom corn and sorghum fields, haystack wagon rides, old-fashioned kids' games in the park, handmade crafts and pioneer demonstrations like blacksmithing, basketmaking, broommaking, weaving, spinning, and more. You also can sample Swedish Beef Soup, a hearty beef-and-vegetable concoction served with hardtack rice pudding and apple cider.

And let's not forget another Christmas celebration: mid-December's Lucia Nights. Every window of the village is lit with a single white candle, and strolling "Santa Lucia" girls wander in and out of the craft shops offering free coffee and cookies; there are also carriage rides through the village and strolling carolers.

Winter

For More Information

For more information and a schedule of events, contact the Bishop Hill State Historic Site, P.O. Box D, Bishop Hill, IL 61419; (309) 927-3345.

42

Treasure Troves

CHICAGO

ARE THE MUMMIES AT THE FIELD MUSEUM GETTING A BIT OLD for you? Do you hate fighting your way through crowds of boom box–blasting teenagers when entering the Museum of Science and Industry, only to find the "working exhibits" broken again? Don't know enough about trendy fashions— and too old to pass for an art student—to make a prime-time appearance at the Art Institute without embarrassing yourself?

Maybe you just need a break from these standard cultural haunts. Or perhaps you should stake out new claims, places that wouldn't automatically come to mind when planning a weekend of museum crawling.

Well, you're in luck. Chicago offers a number of museums that contain treasures far beyond the normal fare. Some might even say they're truly weird. See for yourself.

International Museum of Surgical Science and Hall of Fame 1524 North Lake Shore Drive, Chicago, IL 60610; (312) 642-6502. Free.

Take a leisurely stroll through surgical history at this lakefront mansion with more than 30 rooms. The museum's international exhibits trace the development of surgery through the ages.

And you thought museums were boring!

Old medical instruments (some dating back to Roman times), X-ray equipment, microscopes, and other memorabilia are displayed. My favorite: In the Canada Room, a postmortem plaster cast of the right hand of English novelist William Makepeace Thackeray encased in a red morocco folding case. The original label on the lid reads "A superb Thackeray memento."

And the display on trephination, a form of brain surgery where a hole was poked in the skull, suggests that this may have been the earliest surgical operation performed by prehistoric man.

In fact, you will see some old skulls with quarter-sized holes in them, holes that either "allowed the escape of devils" in patients' heads or were put in doctors' heads by prehistoric patients dissatisfied with the size of their bills.

Oriental Institute, University of Chicago   1155 East 58th Street, Chicago, IL 60637; (773) 702-9521. Free.

Yep, King Tut is here. So is a fragment of the Dead Sea Scrolls. Wrapped and unwrapped mummies, too.

Sorry, no daddies.

This is a fabulous collection of antiquities, with artifacts of every Near East culture dating from 7,000 years ago until the 10th century. In separate galleries, you'll discover art and archaeological treasures from Mesopotamia, Iran, Palestine, Syria, Anatolia, and more.

A 40-ton Assyrian winged bull with a human head is one of my favorites; it once guarded the palace of King Sargon 11 at Khorsabad in 722–705 B.C. So is the 16-foot-tall red quartzite statue of King Tut. Tell me that the 600 B.C. bronze demon figure from Assyria doesn't give you the willies?

And where else can you see a portion of the 2,500-year-old wall (glazed in gold and turquoise) from King Nebuchadnezzar's Babylonian temple?

This museum has only one problem: the museum's name. Ask anyone what you'll find at the Oriental Institute, and they'll say, "Chinese and Japanese stuff." That's because the museum opened in 1919, before the term *Near East* was introduced.

Lizzadro Museum of Lapidary Art   220 Cottage Hill, Elmhurst, IL 60126; (708) 833-1616. Admission.

I'll admit it. I used to impress family and friends by knowing what lapidary art was all about; now everyone knows.

It is the craft of fashioning artworks from raw gemstones. And this museum houses one of the country's most extensive jade and nephrite collections. Twenty-five dioramas, populated with gem-carved figurines, add to the whimsy of the collection. And note the full-size room divider screen and five-piece altar set: they once rested in the Imperial Palace in Beijing.

Bradford Exchange (Museum of Collector's Plates)   9333 North Milwaukee Avenue, Niles, IL 60714; (847) 966-2770. Admission.

My only plate collection reposes in the kitchen sink. But this place is a huge showroom with more than 1,500 limited-edition collector's plates on display in what's been called the world's leading gallery of its kind, valued at nearly a half-million dollars. You'll see everything from Wedgwood to rare and priceless 19th-century collectibles—even plates bearing the likeness of everyone from John Wayne to the Wizard of Oz.

And take a look at the computerized Bradford Exchange trading floor: it resembles the New York Stock Exchange. In fact, museum figures place the worldwide number of plate collectors at more than six million, although I've never personally known even one.

McDonald's Museum   400 North Lee Street, Des Plaines, IL 60016; (847) 297-5022.

How many Big Macs have you wolfed down in your lifetime? If there's some warm spot in your heart (or even if you suffer a bit of heartburn) from your Happy Meal con-

Treasure Troves

sumptions, you might find it interesting to visit the McDonald's Museum in Des Plaines. The 1955-era fast-food palace offers glimpses of original uniforms, equipment, photographs and advertising props, and giveaways that have become a hallmark of McDonald's corporate identity. Just note that if you want to sample another Big Mac, you'll have to head for the Mickey D's across the street.

FOR MORE INFORMATION

For more information about Chicago's little known museums, contact the Illinois Bureau of Tourism, (800) 223-0121.

Winter

43

Bogged Down in Winter

INGLESIDE

IN WINTER, VOLO BOG LOOKS LIKE A LAND THAT TIME forgot. Dry cattails sway in Arctic-like breezes. Leafless brambles huddle in masses as if seeking shelter from biting winds. Tamarack trees are barren and gray.

It is eerie, foreboding, almost lifeless.

Uh-uh.

Take a closer look, say naturalists at the bog. You'll see red berries clinging to the winterberry holly, bright green sphagnum moss everywhere, crinkly red leaves of the leatherleaf, white-winged crossbills cracking open tamarack cones, even the tracks of red fox, weasel, and deer.

Volo Bog, a National Natural Landmark, was carved out of the Chicago region by the last great glacier more than 12,000 years ago, then filled in by melting ice blocks. The bog is an amalgam of conifer needles, leatherleaf, moss, and other decaying debris that eventually forms a floating mat of vegetation.

You've got to get out on the bog to really appreciate its wonders. Walk the bog's half-mile floating boardwalk in winter; you'll notice that, for the most part, the bog surface is frozen solid. But when the thaw comes, you'll graphically see why the wooden trail has been rebuilt at least three times since 1977.

The planks keep sinking due to the wet and unstable peat

soils and fluctuating water levels. Don't be surprised if your weight causes the ground to shake, sway, grind, and vibrate, or if the trail surface sinks below the water level in some spots.

And it's also the only bog in Illinois with open water in the center.

A good place to start your bog adventure is the grand new visitor center, where you can pick up a trail map for self-guided tours; or wait around to join a one-hour, naturalist-led hike rich in bog lore, wildlife tales, and human history stories. These tours are offered year-round on Saturdays and Sundays. (Check with the center for specific times.)

Don't be tempted to touch any of the plant life (which numbers close to 100 species) along the trail; some can be quite nasty to human skin. For example, the sap of poison sumac is, indeed, poisonous to the touch, and contact with ANY portion of the shrub can cause a rash much worse than poison ivy—even in winter.

Other year-round naturalist-led programs make the bog an interesting place to spend part of any weekend. A hawk-watching program is offered in November; "Winter on the Prairie" and "The Lost Oceans of Northeast Illinois" (both held in mid-February) are a couple of special winter events that bring the bog to life during the cold season. In warm weather, the bog explodes with all kinds of color, including blossoming wildflowers ranging from marsh marigolds to wild orchids.

FOR MORE INFORMATION

Admission to Volo Bog is free. Guided tours are offered Saturdays and Sundays. Call ahead for winter and summer park and visitor center hours. For more information, contact the Volo Bog State Natural Area, 28478 West Brandenburg Road, Ingleside, IL 60041; (815) 344-1294.

44

Lights, Camera, Holiday Action

FINDLAY, BELLEVILLE, EAST PEORIA

IF YOU WANT TO BRIGHTEN UP YOUR HOLIDAY SEASON, WHY not come up with some illuminating idea of your own? Or maybe you'd just rather head to one of Illinois's yuletide lights festivals, where you can wander grounds crammed with fabulous electro-sculpture light displays that include everything from 30-foot-tall wooden soldiers to a lighted, drive-thru holiday tunnel.

Here are the best and the brightest of the bunch.

Lake Shelbyville Festival of Lights During the Lake Shelbyville Festival of Lights in Findlay, early November through mid-January, nearly two-and-a-half-million winking and blinking electric lights create America's second-largest holiday light show.

The award-winning Illinois bash, which draws more than 200,000 Yuletide fans to its three-month run, is surpassed only by a similar extravaganza in Wheeling, West Virginia. But being second biggest doesn't seem to bother any of the families that drive through a three-mile-long "holiday tunnel" into themed Christmas scenes ablaze with twinkling lights.

Headquartered in Eagle Creek State Park, the festival features more than 200 Santa-inspired displays lining the auto route from the shores of Lake Shelbyville into the deep woods. There are also free pony rides for the kids, as well as live entertainment. "Toyland" is a kids' favorite lighted theme village. Wooden soldiers nearly 30 feet tall, candy canes, snowmen, trumpeting angels, and a sweeping canopy of twinkling lights add to the holiday merriment.

Kids also can tour the village for free in the bed of a hay-wagon, while adults may choose to cuddle inside a carriage pulled by Clydesdale horses. (There is a fee for carriage rides.)

To make a weekend of it, consider overnighting in the Inn at Eagle Creek Resort. The woodland setting is magnificent, the inn decor is French Country, the accommodations are luxurious, and the restaurant serves good food. This elegant lodge has 128 rooms, a glassed-in indoor pool so you can peek out at the winter wonderland landscape, a fitness facility with whirlpool and sauna, and cross-country ski trails.

Several packages are available, including a "lights" special offering one night's lodging, breakfast (for two), a hayride through the lighted theme villages, and a souvenir mug; children under 18 stay free in the same room as their parents. For more information, call (800) 874-3529 or (217) 774-2244.

Annual Way of Lights   The Annual Way of Lights, the first Saturday after Thanksgiving through the Feast of the Epiphany at the National Shrine of Our Lady of the Snows in Belleville, claims to be the country's first-ever large-scale holiday lights display. It remains one of the biggest, featuring a two-mile-long "lights drive" illuminated by more than 300,000 lights; two new "light tunnels"; and five custom-made, cutting-edge "electro-light sculptures" depicting the story of the journey to Bethlehem and the birth of the Christ child.

Winter

The free festival also boasts horse-drawn carriage rides through the lights displays and open-air tram rides (both Mondays through Thursdays only), a live animal corral, and area choirs performing all sorts of Christmas songs. Inside, kids' activities include a coloring room, video games, puppet shows, face painting—even a Christmas gift store where children can purchase $1 presents for Mom and Dad.

Let's not forget the shrine's Christmas tree festival. It features 12 trees decorated in distinct ethnic immigrant styles. One year more than 350,000 people made their way through the holiday lights displays. So I guess the two months that it takes workers here to put up the displays are well worth the effort. Call (618) 397-6700.

Festival of Lights/Parade of Lights More than five million holiday lights shine out at East Peoria's annual Festival of Lights/Parade of Lights, late November through December. That's a light for just about everybody in the entire city—or at least, everybody that has anything to do with this bright idea.

The festival kicks off with an opening day (or should I say night) lighted parade at 6:00 P.M. More than 50 illuminated floats, ranging from golf-cart size to 70 feet long, rumble through downtown streets in front of an expected crowd of 100,000 people.

Then wander through several theme areas with more holiday lights displays. Newest is Winter Wonderland, a two-mile-long driveway complete with about 30 lighted archways, whose light decorations include everything from prehistoric animals to space shuttles. The Enchanted Forest offers more than 700 lighted trees, Christmas trees that talk to visitors, and Santa. Then there's Folepi's Marketplace, featuring 140 craft booths.

If you'd rather leave the driving to others, hop aboard a bus for a guided tour; there is an admission fee for adults and kids taking the bus tour. Call (309) 699-6212.

For More Information

For more Christmas lights festival information, contact the Illinois Bureau of Tourism, (800) 223-0121.

Winter

45

Where Eagles Dare

ROCK ISLAND

IT'S A SIGHT THAT NEVER CEASES TO AMAZE ME WITH ITS beauty and majesty. A bald eagle swoops and swirls high over the Mississippi River. Suddenly the bird dives, talons extended, to snatch a fish from the frigid waters of the river's ice-choked channels.

Then the eagle glides to its nest in a lofty tree along the craggy bluff-filled riverbank to feed and rest before starting its hunting cycle all over again.

Yep, America's feathered trademark is the star of Bald Eagle Days in the Quad Cities, an annual late-January/early-February festival headquartered in Rock Island. The two-day nature extravaganza features everything from close-up looks at live eagles and lectures by eagle experts to an indoor environmental fair with exhibits by national conservation organizations like the Sierra Club, Audubon Society, National Wildlife Federation, and local conservation groups.

Site for all the indoor programs is the Quad City Expo Center, and admission is free.

But the biggest thrill of all is getting out on the roads and into the fields along the river to use spotting scopes set up by naturalists (or your own binoculars) and watch these birds of prey in flight.

The U.S. Army Corps of Engineers reports that, from mid-December through February, as many as 1,500

American bald eagles winter on the Mississippi between Minneapolis and St. Louis.

Eagles summer in Canada and the northern states, then migrate south to the Quad Cities as the river freezes. Locks and dams keep the Mississippi from completely icing over in spots, allowing the birds to feed on their primary winter food source—fish.

Your best chance to see an eagle might be at Sunset Park in Rock Island. A ranger from the Army Corp of Engineers and conservation-group volunteers are on hand with spotting scopes for bird-watchers. They'll also happily answer questions about the birds and their habitat.

Eagle-watching can be done solo from one of the Quad Cities' public observation areas. Locations include the Rock Island riverfront, downstream of Lock and Dam 15; the Davenport, Iowa, riverfront, also downstream of Lock and Dam 15; the south entrance of Fisherman's Corner, off Illinois 84 at Lock and Dam 14 near Hampton; Credit Island, accessible from Iowa 61 south of Davenport; and Iowa's Pleasant Valley at Lock and Dam 14.

Prime spotting spots beyond the Quad Cities include Lock and Dam 13 in Fulton, Illinois; Lock and Dam 16, across from Muscatine, Iowa; and Lock and Dam 19 in Keokuk, Iowa. Maps pinpointing eagle-watching hot spots are available at the Expo Center.

Eagle-watchers should be sure to wear heavy winter clothing, including hat, gloves, and insulated boots. The Corps of Engineers also cautions visitors to stay far enough away from the eagles so that they aren't frightened into flight.

The birds endure considerable stress from cold temperatures and need rest to conserve energy that maintains body heat. They are frightened of humans and can spot you with eyes nearly six times as powerful as

Winter

yours. So stay as quiet as possible; even the slam of a single car door can set them off.

FOR MORE INFORMATION

Overnight eagle-watching packages are available from local hotels, motels, and bed and breakfasts. For more eagle-watching details, contact the Quad Cities Convention and Visitors Bureau, (800) 747-7800.

Where Eagles Dare

46

Time Travels

ROCKFORD

YOU CAN'T CLIMB ABOARD A TIME MACHINE, STEP THROUGH a time warp, or "beam up" to another dimension in order to journey back through history.

At least, not yet.

But you can visit the Time Museum, located appropriately enough in Rockford's Clock Tower Inn, for a fascinating look at the history of time measurement.

The Time Museum houses a world-class collection of almost 3,000 timekeeping devices dating from 2000 B.C. to today. In fact, it's one of the most comprehensive gatherings of timekeeping contraptions currently in existence—featuring everything from the smallest spring-driven clock to massive wooden and mechanical structures.

You can walk through 14 "time salons," each featuring a period in the evolution of clocks and timepieces. From Stonehenge to the atomic-powered clock, the displays include sundials, astrolabes, nocturnals, compendiums, incense-burning clocks, water clocks, sandglasses, weight clocks, calendars, chronometers, fire clocks, navigational devices . . .

Whew! Gimme a minute to catch my breath.

There's also a large collection of "performing clocks." A

"piano clock" plays portions of Mozart's *Magic Flute* every hour. An ornate French "bird cage clock," built in 1834, boasts eight small mechanical birds chirping at the strike of the hour. And a larger timepiece (said to have been built for Napoleon, who then presented it to a Turkish sultan) depicts an actual naval battle complete with mechanical ships riding the ocean's swells.

Other timepieces include 19th-century Chinese pocket sundials carved of ivory, a dazzling silver clock studded with rubies, and a tiny time gadget invented by Benjamin Franklin.

And while some of the most famous clockmakers in history are represented by their finest works, the masterpiece of the collection (and a visitor favorite) remains an imposing clock made in Germany by Christian Gebhard and his two sons.

This time device took 30 years to complete. Working almost full-time on the clock from 1865 to 1895, the Gebhards created a masterpiece, nearly 12 feet tall and 8 feet wide, that colorfully illustrates basic astronomical configurations.

But far more interesting is the performance given every 15 minutes by the clock's numerous mechanical figures. The main activity takes place at noon, when the figure of an old man strikes the quarter hours, a skeleton tolls the hours, an angel turns an hourglass to signify the passing of time, and the 12 Apostles revolve around a figure of Christ. Judas turns his back on the Christ figure while clutching a bag of silver, and a cock crows three times at the appearance of Peter—signifying his "apocryphal" denial of Christ after the prophet's arrest.

And every year at midnight, January 1, a trumpeter emerges from the top of the clock to herald the New Year.

As you'll discover, time rarely stands still at the Time Museum.

Winter

For More Information

Guided tours, offered on weekends, add to an understanding of the workings of the museum's time devices; it's best to call ahead for tour reservations. The Clock Tower Inn also offers overnight packages. For more information, contact the Time Museum, 7801 East State Street, Rockford, IL 61101; (815) 398-6000.

Time Travels

47

Downhill Thrills

It doesn't have the back bowls of Vail. You won't be rubbing elbows with celebrities. And the maximum vertical of 475 feet would be a mere pimple on the Rocky Mountain landscape.

But Illinois does have skiing, and thanks to giant snow-makers, the season starts going downhill by mid-December.

If you'd like to try the flatlanders' version of schussing, here are the skiing hot spots:

Chestnut Mountain Eight miles south of Galena in north-west Illinois, Chestnut Mountain is the Land of Lincoln's only downhill ski lodge and resort, so you might as well enjoy it. Luckily, it's a beauty.

Cut into the high, tree-topped limestone bluffs that tum-ble down to the Mississippi River, Chestnut Mountain's 230 acres of skiing include 17 runs (the longest more than a half-mile long) and the state's biggest vertical drop—475 feet. While this might appear negligible to Colorado-hopping vet-erans, it remains quite impressive for the Midwest—and translates into plenty of downhill thrills.

Chestnut Mountain has other selling points. Ski runs are lighted nightly until 10:00 P.M. The cost of lift tickets won't set you back a second mortgage. More than 20 snowmaking machines provide powder even in the most erratic winter weather. And the resort's lodge is first-rate, with nearly 150 guest rooms, 3 restaurants, live entertainment, and an indoor swimming pool.

How about these other après-skiing adventures? A short drive away is historic Galena, a lead-mining boomtown that in winter resembles a Currier and Ives print come to life. Turn-of-the-century architecture, craft shops, art galleries, terrific restaurants, and antiques are the attractions here along with President U. S. Grant's post–Civil War home. And several historic bed and breakfasts offer ski packages.

Snowstar Ski Area About seven miles southwest of Rock Island, Snowstar Ski Area offers 13 ski runs ranging from beginner to expert. But the emphasis here is on family skiing, not hot-dogging. Especially popular is the one-day beginner's package, which includes lessons and rental equipment. Area motels also offer skiers' packages or discounts. Call (800) 383-4002.

Chicago Skiing If you've just got to ski, but want to be near the world-class amenities of the Windy City, you're also in luck.

Five Chicago-area ski operations offer nearby downhill thrills without the usual long-distance highway hassles. Some are only minutes from downtown Chicago; others are just across the Illinois-Wisconsin border, about an hour or so from the city.

Of course, all these ski areas offer modest slopes at best. But, hey. At least you'll get to strap on the skis, feel the winter wind burn your face, and zoom down "mountain powder." Among the best are:

- Villa Olivia Ski Area, State 20, Bartlett, IL; (630) 289-5200. Many of my friends had their first downhill thrills at this suburban ski hill. It has 12 runs, with an extremely modest vertical of 180 feet and one trail that stretches about a half-mile. This place has been called a real ego builder for beginners. Rentals, ski lessons for adults, and kids' programs are available.

- Wilmot Mountain, Wilmot, Wisconsin; (414) 862-2301. This is where I first skied, and it continues to draw swarms of beginners, especially on weekends. But it also challenges with a few intermediate runs like Little Superior and Snow Bowl. And a couple of mogul trails add excitement to this little gem. Oh yes, there are 25 runs, and the vertical is 230 feet.

- Alpine Valley, East Troy, Wisconsin; (414) 642-7374. With a vertical of 388 feet, this might be the highest hill near Chicago. Among its 12 runs, Big Thunder has moguls lined up from top to bottom. There also are several intermediate and "advanced" slopes.

Other ski hopefuls include:

- Americana Ski Area, State 50, Lake Geneva, Wisconsin; (414) 248-8811

- Four Lakes Ski Area, Lisle, IL; (630) 964-2550

Downhill Thrills

For More Information

For more Chestnut Mountain ski information (including ski/lodging packages), contact Chestnut Mountain, Box 328, Galena, IL 61036; (800) 397-1320. To get Galena-related ski package information, call the Galena/Jo Daviess Office of Tourism, (800) 747-9377. For other Illinois ski information, contact the Illinois Bureau of Tourism, (800) 223-0121.

48

Tour-Riffic Chicago

CHICAGO LOVES TO SHOW OFF.

And one of the best ways for weekenders to get a handle on all the Windy City has to offer is by signing up for a guided tour that puts a new focus on its surroundings. Of course, I'm not talking about those general sightseeing bus tours that hit a hundred city highlights in an hour or so, leaving its passengers floundering in a whirlwind of dates, trivia, and really bad jokes.

Instead, hop aboard a tour that examines one special facet of the country's third-largest burg. There are scores of special-interest tours worth considering, and they cover the gamut of subjects—from architecture to the "Untouchables."

Here are a few of the best:

Architectural Tours   Bright lights, big city, tall buildings . . . really tall buildings, really old buildings, really unusual buildings, buildings designed by some of the world's most celebrated architects. If you're bonkers over buildings, the Chicago Architecture Foundation offers almost 60 different tours covering just about every Chicago neighborhood and noteworthy architectural feature.

You can zoom to the top of the Sears Tower (the world's tallest building); look at the Louis Sullivan–designed Carson Pirie Scott Building; visit the historic Rookery; peek inside

Frank Lloyd Wright's home in Oak Park; even view Bertrand Goldberg's "River City" development, which one architecture critic has dubbed "Jetsons-esque," after TV's cartoon space-age family.

If you'd rather see Chicago's skyline architecture by boat, sign up for the Architecture River Cruise, which floats down the Chicago River in the shadows of downtown's tall skyscrapers. Or perhaps the "Chicago Movie Palaces" tour, a four-hour ride/walk through some of the city's grandest theaters, is more to your liking? You can get more information at the Architecture Foundation's headquarters, 224 South Michigan Avenue; call (312) 922-8687.

Supernatural Tours   If you like things that go bump in the night, then a "Supernatural Tour" might set you howling like a werewolf. Led by professional ghostbusters who have tracked down all kinds of spooky spirits, you'll be whisked through the night to some of the city's most famous haunts—including creepy cemeteries and doppelganger-infested houses. Of course, you're likely to hear about "Resurrection Mary," perhaps Chicago's most renowned (and seen?) ghost. Call (708) 499-0300.

Chicago Sun-Times   Want to see how big-time reporters do their jobs at one of the country's largest newspapers? Just head to the *Chicago Sun-Times*, whose 500,000-plus daily circulation ranks it about 10th biggest in the country. Tour both its newsroom and sports department, where you can watch journalists peck on their computer keyboards as they write about the day's most exciting events.

You'll also get to walk along a long glass-walled hallway that exposes the paper's huge, deafening (and quite old) printing presses; watch as gigantic rolls of newsprint make their way through scores of press machines as ink-stained pressmen scurry to keep things moving and get the latest edition out on the streets. Call (312) 321-3251.

Winter

Greektown Here's a self-guided tour that'll having you crying "Opaa" all night. Just head to Greektown (basically Jackson and Halsted on Chicago's Near West Side), and you'll be instantly transported into a Zorba the Greek world of *saganaki*, flaming foods, and maybe even a belly dancer or two.

First stop is The Parthenon, a Greektown restaurant landmark, which claims it invented the flaming cheese pie. Also try its Greek salad, roast leg of lamb, *moussaka*, and more. Greek music plays quietly in the background.

Not so quiet is Neon Greek Village, just down the street, an authentic Greek nightclub that caters to lovers of belly dancing and good food. Look above you—that's supposed to be the blue Greek sky overhead. Two movies have been shot at Dianna's Opaa, another feted restaurant located nearby. And of all the eateries, Greek Islands might be the best. Food, ambiance (there's even a balcony or kitchen garden dining area), and music are extravagant. Sample the *tarmasalada* (fish roe) and *tzatziki* (yogurt, cucumbers, and garlic) for appetizers; then move on to a zesty Greek salad before ravishing unequaled lamb chops or fresh fish like sea bass or red snapper. Top all of it off with Cava Cambas Greek white wine, and you're in heaven.

Finally, if you're looking for romance, head to Pegasus, which boasts Greektown's only restaurant roof garden—and claims to have been the love magnet that has led to more than 5,000 weddings. Bachelors and bachelorettes—enter at your own risk.

Four final suggestions: You can visit more than 20 important sites of African American history on American Tour and Travel's Heritage Tour; call (312) 978-8900. Tour the Chicago Board of Trade; guides at its fifth-floor visitor center will tell you why all those screaming, gesticulating futures traders (dressed in green, blue, and yellow jackets) look like they're about to start a riot; call (312) 435-3590.

Tour-Riffic Chicago

If you'd like a bird's-eye view of the John Hancock Building, call Allegra's Aircraft and Helicopter Tours. It's not only visually stimulating, but you'll easily recognize the grid system that was used to platt the city of Chicago; call (312) 735-4440. Or head to the *Chicago Tribune*'s Freedom Center for a tour of its sophisticated new printing plant. Audio "wands" at various stations in the plant allow you to hear descriptions of activities in production, shipping, warehousing, and delivery. Upon completion of your visit, you'll receive a set of the *Trib*'s 20 most famous front pages; call (312) 222-2116.

FOR MORE INFORMATION

For more information about Chicago tours and Greektown restaurants, contact the Chicago Office of Tourism, (312) 744-2400.

Winter

49

A Final Yule Fling— with a French Accent

ELLIS GROVE

IF YOU'RE LUCKY ENOUGH TO LIVE IN ILLINOIS, ONE OF YOUR final chances to celebrate the holiday season with that certain joie de vivre comes with a French accent.

Head to the Twelfth Day of Christmas Celebration, slated in early January at the Pierre Menard State Historic Site in the southwestern portion of the state. You'll be in for a lively afternoon of French songs and dances, samples of colonial-style French pastries, and tours of the vintage home led by guides dressed in period costumes.

Built in 1800 by Illinois's first lieutenant governor, the Menard House has been called the finest example of southern French Colonial architecture in the Mississippi Valley. It is adorned, this time of year, with holiday finery that typified upper-class French life in North America two centuries ago.

But do not expect to see a Christmas tree among all the seasonal decorations. In colonial times, the French didn't put up holiday trees, explains a site interpreter. Their biggest celebration was held on the Twelfth Day of Christmas (January 6), when the Wise Men are said to have discovered the Christ child in Bethlehem. So you'll see the home's nativity scene instead.

Also count on mouthwatering aromas. That's because visitors will be treated to home-baked madeleines (delectable French pastries), yule logs (rolled chocolate cakes), and French cookies, along with coffee and punch.

You can work off your indulgences by dancing a minuet and singing lively French Christmas songs. Or tour the handsome home, filled with Menard family heirlooms.

Another option is a walk along the 187 stone steps behind the house that lead to Fort Kaskaskia State Historic Site, once a French outpost on the Mississippi River. Rather than allowing the British to occupy the fort during the French and Indian War, townspeople burned it to the ground in 1765. Remaining are earthworks surrounding the old fort's perimeter. Next to the fort is Garrison Hill Cemetery, a pioneer graveyard.

For even more French history, drive 20 miles northwest to Fort de Chartres State Historic Site in Prairie du Rocher. Once the strongest fortress in the Mississippi River Valley, the great stone structure was built in 1756. The north wall and guardhouse have been reconstructed, and the Peithman Museum displays French-period artifacts.

FOR MORE INFORMATION

Admission to the Twelfth Day of Christmas Celebration is free. The Menard House is located off County 1; for hours, directions, and other information, contact the Pierre Menard Home State Historic Site, 4230 Kaskaskia Road, Ellis Grove, IL 62241, (618) 859-3031; for Fort de Chartres State Historic Site information, call (618) 284-7230.

Winter

50

Chicago's Cultural Gems

"WOW! SEE THAT, PA?" ASKED MY DAUGHTER KATE, AS THE dolphin shot out of the water in a high arc before plunging back into the pool with a giant splash.

"It's just like Sea World!"

Well, not quite. Chicago's Shedd Aquarium is much better.

But the Shedd is only one of the city's three cultural attractions—the aquarium, Adler Planetarium, and the Field Museum of Natural History—found within a one-mile crescent along Lake Michigan.

It could take a month's worth of weekends to properly explore these treasure troves of history, knowledge, and wonderment. Here's some help: a thumbnail guide to these three visitors' paradises, including some "shouldn't-miss" highlights for each of them.

John G. Shedd Aquarium The John G. Shedd Aquarium is the world's largest, offering a fascinating glimpse into the realm of underwater creatures and their natural habitats of oceans and lakes.

Its most fabulous attraction is a $43 million saltwater oceanarium, completed in 1991, which resembles a rocky Pacific Northwest oceanside harbor. Surrounding the spectacular 170,000-square-foot setting is a 1,000-seat amphitheater, from which visitors watch 20-minute naturalist-led marine life presentations featuring Pacific white-sided dolphins. Yet another 40,000-gallon, two-level tank contains beluga whales, false killer whales, harbor seals, and Alaskan sea otters (many of them rescued from the *Exxon Valdez* oil spill of 1989).

Another fascinating display is the aquarium's $1.2 million saltwater "Coral Reef," a 90,000-gallon tank (12 feet deep and 40 feet in diameter), containing 500 Caribbean fish and colorful coral rocks, sea sponges, sea fans, and more.

Feeding time (twice daily) at the Coral Reef creates great theater. A scuba diver equipped with a microphone device hand-feeds all kinds of fish while talking to spectators—who even get to ask the diver questions. Count on seeing barracuda, triggerfish, groupers, moray eels—even sharks! And let's not forget "Dead Eye," a tarpon blind in one eye who has been at the aquarium since 1935.

Even after all this, you still have more than 200 exhibit tanks to view, featuring about 7,000 fish representing more than 700 saltwater and freshwater species. For more information, contact John G. Shedd Aquarium, 1200 South Lake Shore Drive, Chicago, IL 60605; (312) 939-2426.

Adler Planetarium The Adler Planetarium and Astronomy Museum, located just down a winding path east of the aquarium, was the first of its kind to be built in the Western Hemisphere. Constructed in 1930 on an island about a half-mile out in Lake Michigan, it is connected to the mainland by a city-constructed peninsula.

The planetarium offers all kinds of spacy fun. You'll see a solar system in 3-D, space equipment, lunar modules, even a live hookup to outer space via an observing telescope located in New Mexico. Another display features the telescope that discovered the planet Uranus.

But my favorite exhibit might be the 74-gram, four-billion-year-old moon rock, collected by astronaut David Scott on the Apollo 15 mission.

The mainstay of the planetarium's special programming is its Sky Shows, whose topics change every few months.

Among the favorites are "Secrets of the Ancient Skywatchers" (astronomy in the primitive world), "Fast Forward to the Future" (a look at life 500 years from now), and the "Star of Wonder" (an enormously popular Christmas presentation). There are also kids' shows on Saturday and Sunday mornings.

Come to a Friday Sky Show if you'd like to see images of planets, stars, and galaxies projected onto the Sky Theater dome from the Doane Observatory's 20-inch computer-controlled telescope; this way all 430 people in the theater can simultaneously view solar system objects millions of light-years away. Contact the Adler Planetarium, 1300 South Lake Shore Drive, Chicago, IL 60605; (312) 922-7827.

Field Museum of Natural History Brachiosaurus, the world's largest mounted dinosaur (it stands nearly four stories tall), greets you at the Field Museum of Natural History, located just across Lake Shore Drive from the aquarium and planetarium in the city's "cultural crescent." But this is only the beginning of awe-inducing discoveries at the museum, where more than 19 million artifacts are displayed in a world-renowned collection that sprawls over nine acres of exhibit space—including the newest dino discovery, Sue the T-Rex!

Don't think that this is one of those musty repositories where professorial types whisper in hushed tones about boring exhibits. On the contrary, this is a "museum that rocks," where visitors are likely to hear native chants, animal roars, and birdcalls, and see fast-moving video displays. There's even a special kids' museum-within-a-museum hands-on exhibit where little ones can do everything from touching the tooth of a woolly mammoth to petting a polar bear.

One of my favorite displays is the Egyptian tomb. Actually, it's a reconstruction of the tomb of King Unis-Ankh, last pharaoh of the Fifth Dynasty (2428–2407 B.C.). Even though I've walked through here scores of times, I still get

Chicago's Cultural Gems

the willies; imagine how those early Egyptologists must have felt when they were exploring real pharaonic tombs in the Near East.

The display includes the pharaoh's burial chamber, and it leads to the museum's vast collection of real mummies— caught in various stages of unwrapping.

Contact the Field Museum of Natural History, Roosevelt Road at Lake Shore Drive, Chicago, IL 60605; (312) 922-9410.

FOR MORE INFORMATION

For more information about Chicago's major museums, contact the Chicago Office of Tourism, Chicago Cultural Center, (312) 744-2400.

Winter

51

Gonna Pump You Up

GILMAN

LOOKING FOR A GOOD WORKOUT?

How about a wellness center that addresses fitness from a holistic perspective?

Maybe you just want to go somewhere for a weekend and be pampered?

Look no farther than the Heartland Spa in Gilman, named one of the 25 best spas in the world by Condé Nast's *Traveler* magazine. Located amid cornfields and cow pastures on 31 peaceful acres of the Kam Lake Estate, the retreatlike setting allows guests to relax and concentrate on their individual fitness goals in a high-tech exercise environment that remains Midwest friendly and unpretentious.

How unpretentious? The exercise salon is located in a converted barn. But don't let looks fool you; this is a state-of-the-art wellness environment complete with indoor pool, weight room, cardiovascular room, hayloft aerobics studio, and 32 different kinds of fitness classes—from "aqua motion" in-water aerobics to tai chi chuan.

Let's not forget the ultimate indulgence: spa pampering that extends to full-body sea-salt exfoliation, Swiss collagen-elastin facials, and honey-mud masques, as well as body composition analysis, inner diet assessment, and personal nutrition counseling sessions.

New guests start out with a tour of the grounds, which includes a three-acre private lake. The main lodge is a large white country house nestled near the water's edge. You'll learn that you don't even need a change of clothes here: the spa provides everybody with an egalitarian set of exercise duds that includes a pair of slippers.

It's also explained that you can keep very busy during your stay (workout weekends are most popular) or do nothing at all. Stay in your room, if you like. It's up to you.

Also note that food is available 24 hours a day. Of course, food means fruits, vegetables, and beverages like coffee and tea (no alcohol).

But don't get the wrong idea about Heartland's spa cuisine. It's healthy but quite tasty, since the executive chef works with a registered dietitian to come up with a choice of low-fat but fun foods. Like black-bean burritos with cucumber-and-pepper relish and mock sour cream.

It's up to you to schedule a workout regimen. I especially like the "Boxercise" class for a workout with some punch. It incorporates basic boxing moves (footwork and handwork) with aerobic and anaerobic exercises. It's tough, "but you come out feeling like a champ."

Another interesting choice is Wushu or Kung Fu. No, Grasshopper, this may be a martial art that teaches self-defense, but it also provides exercise for the mind. By learning form, proper stance, and blocking movements, you can improve your coordination, reflex response, and concentration.

And during winter, you can walk out the door and schuss the spa's cross-country ski trails. It's still the best aerobic exercise known to humankind.

Newest wrinkle in Heartland's wellness program is the "Heartland Adventure," a mini Outward Bound–like personal challenge that can include everything from scaling 12-foot walls to leaping for a trapeze 30 feet in the air.

For More Information

Weekend, five-night, and seven-night programs are offered. Heartland Spa is located about 80 miles south of Chicago. For more information, contact The Heartland Spa, Corporate Office, 225 North Wabash Avenue, Suite 310, Chicago, IL 60601; (312) 357-6465.

Gonna Pump You Up

52

The Wright Stuff

WISCONSIN ALWAYS BRAGS THAT IT HAS THE "WRIGHT STUFF."
Wrong.

Renowned architect Frank Lloyd Wright designed his first house in River Forest in 1893. His magnificent home and studio are located in Oak Park, where he practiced from 1898 to 1909.

In fact, Oak Park has a higher concentration of Wright structures than anywhere else in the world, claiming 25 in all. Neighboring River Forest counts eight more. And you'll find a number of Wright designs in Chicago and around the state, too.

So let's put to rest the notion that Wright's legacy is exclusively a Wisconsin bragging right. Illinois possesses some of the architect's greatest landmarks.

Here's a Land of Lincoln guide to some of Wright's masterpieces.

Frank Lloyd Wright Home and Studio   Oak Park has been called "a remarkable outdoor museum of architecture," thanks to its collection of 25 Frank Lloyd Wright–designed buildings. It's here that the maverick Midwest genius broke down pretentious European standards of design; in fact, he shattered all the rules, developing his Prairie style of low, earth-hugging dwellings that changed the course of 20th-century architecture.

Fitting for a man who said, "The book of creation is my [architectural] textbook."

Any Wright Heritage Trail tour should start at the Frank Lloyd Wright Home and Studio, 951 Chicago Avenue, Oak Park, IL 60302; (708) 848-1976. Wright built this architectural gem in 1889, when he was only 22 years old. Note the front of the home's exterior: How many geometric shapes can you spot? This is evidence of Wright's already developing fascination with combining shapes and structures to complement (or blend into) natural surroundings.

In fact, it was said that "this house began to associate with the ground and become natural to its prairie state."

Inside, note that the entry room, living room, and study have wide openings; all the rooms are connected yet separate. In the middle of this cluster of rooms is the fireplace, which Wright considered the heart of the home. It consists of exposed masonry (unlike most homes of the day whose fireplaces were adorned with all kinds of woods, tiles, and delicate coverings). Wright wanted the house's natural materials to come right into the living space and be "solid like the earth." Even the dining room floor is covered with red clay.

Horizontal lines are everywhere; and the house contains some walls that do not connect to the ceiling—or even another wall. Wright said that his "sense of a wall was no longer the side of a box . . . it was to bring the outside world into the house and let the inside of the house go outside."

Especially noteworthy is the children's playroom, with its 15-foot-high barrel vault ceiling, "built-in" grand piano, and double balcony. Again, geometric shapes are everywhere— the barrel ceiling, arches, ceiling grille, bookcases. Why was the playroom so important? Wright and his wife raised six children in this house.

And see how form follows function in Wright's choice of squares and rectangles within octagons in the library.

Wright's studio also gives a fascinating glimpse into his design philosophy. Would you have built "around" the willow tree, allowing it to grow "through" the house? And the drafting room's balcony is really suspended by chains from the roof beam.

Throw in all the Wright-designed furniture, stained glass, and other organically rooted accessories, and you'll begin to understand what Wright meant when he said, "All these things [the building, furnishings, and settings] work together as one thing."

Unity Temple   Another Oak Park Wright building worth visiting is the Unity Temple at 875 Lake Street. It's been called Wright's "little jewel box." Designed in 1905, the Prairie Style masterpiece, made from a revolutionary concrete design, is said to be the only major public structure from the architect's early days that's still used today. Call (708) 383-8873.

Frederick C. Robie House   The Frederick C. Robie House, 5757 S. Woodlawn, Chicago, IL 60637, (773) 834-1847, has been called the "quintessential Prairie House." Wright designed every nook and cranny of this 1910 masterpiece, which many consider the culmination of his visionary architectural innovations. In typical Wright fashion, its rooms cluster around the hearth; its wide roof overhangs; and horizontal bands of limestone and intricate brickwork echo the low horizontal planes of the flatlands.

Inside, the Robie House "seems as much a work of nature as art." Natural materials are used everywhere, including unpainted brick and lots of natural oak; even exposed rough plaster never looked so good.

You'll also be flabbergasted to note that the entire house cost $57,500—$14,500 for the corner lot, $35,000 for the house, and $8,000 for custom furnishings.

Dana-Thomas House State Historic Site 301 East
Lawrence Avenue, Springfield, IL 62703, (217) 782-6776,
claims to be the "best preserved and most complete" of
Frank Lloyd Wright's early Prairie homes. Completed in
1904, it swallowed up the preexisting Italianate family home
of socialite Susan Lawrence Dana, who gave Wright carte
blanche to restructure the residence. The house evidences
all of the architect's most characteristic features—low horizontal roofs, wide overhanging eaves, rows of ribbon art
glass.

The Dana-Thomas House also boasts more than 200
pieces of original Wright-designed white oak furniture; 250
art-glass door, window, and light panels; and more than 200
original light fixtures and skylights. No wonder it is considered such a treasure.

Among the scores of details worth noting are the
Lawrence Avenue front arched entryway framing an original terra-cotta sculpture by Richard Bock (a friend and col-
laborator of Wright's) and the dining room, with its intricate
Wright-designed butterfly light fixture.

Other Wright designs in Illinois include the following:

- In downtown Chicago (at 209 South LaSalle), Wright
  remodeled the Rookery Building's lobby. Note his trademark geometric designs and suspended chandeliers and
  light fixtures.

- The Petit Memorial Chapel in Belvidere was built in the
  early 1900s. The tiny, wood-trimmed chapel was a gathering place for both funeral services and before inter-
  ments. Call (815) 547-7642.

- Wright even designed banks—like the one in Dwight. Its
  boxy spaces can be absorbed only during business hours.
  Call (815) 584-1212.

FOR MORE INFORMATION

For more Wright information, contact the Oak Park Visitors Center, 158 Forest Avenue, Oak Park, IL 60602, 708-848-1500; and the Illinois Bureau of Tourism, (800) 223-0121.

241

The Wright Stuff

Index

Abraham Lincoln Association
    Banquet, 33
Adler Planetarium, 230–31
African American historic sites, 103–7
African American history, 225
African World Festival, 107
Aldrich Guest House, 101, 164
Alpine Valley, 221
Alton, 149, 162
Alton Belle Riverboat, 149, 164
American Ski Area, 221
Amish settlements, 153–57
Annual Way of Lights, 208–9
Antiques, 47–48
Apple picking, 137–39
Aquariums, 229–30
Architectural tours, 223–24
Architecture River Cruise, 224
Arcola, 156–57
Arthur, 155–56
Aurora, 70, 106, 150
Autumn on Parade festival, 188–89

Baha'i House of Worship, 9–10
Banks, Ernie, 36
Barn tours, 23
Bartlett, 220
Batcolumn, 36
Beer Nuts, Inc., 25
Bell Smith Springs, 176
Belleville, 208–9
Billy Goat Tavern, 11
Bishop Hill, 197–200
Black Pioneers Exhibit, 105
Bloomington, 25, 45–46
Bowling alleys, 21–22
Bradford Exchange, 203
Bundling Board Inn, 94–95
Burdick, Sharon, 188

Cahokia, 105, 162–63
Cahokia Mounds Museum Society, 172
Cahokia Mounds State Historic Site,
    89–91, 162, 164
Calder, Alexander, 38
Canoeing, 127–33
Carbondale, 173
Carthage, 161, 164
Casino Queen, The, 150
Casino Rock Island, 148
Casinos, 70, 147–52

Cave-in-Rock, 111–12, 114, 175
Cave-in-Rock State Park, 111, 114
Chagall, Marc, 36–37
Channahon State Park, 128–29, 179
Cheese plants, 23
Chesterton, Ind., 71
Chestnut Mountain, 219–20
Chicago, 10–12, 35–39, 201–4, 220–21,
    223–26, 229–32
Chicago Bears summer training camp,
    83–84
Chicago Board of Trade, 225
Chicago Botanic Gardens, 28–29
Chicago Portage National Historic Site,
    178
Chicago Sun-Times, 11, 224
Chicago Tribune, 11, 226
Chicagoland Canoe Base, 133
Christmas lights festivals, 207–10
City of Lights I and II riverboat casinos,
    150
Clock Tower Inn, 217
Collectibles, 47–48
Collector's Plates, Museum of, 203
Collinsville, 89–91, 162
Colonnade Apartments, 13–14
Crab Orchard Lake, 173–74
Creekwood Inn, 72
Cuneo, John, 55–56
Cuneo Museum, 55–57

Dana-Thomas House State Historic
    Site, 240
Debs, Eugene, 12–13
Decatur, 23, 34
DeKalb, 118
Des Plaines River, 132
DeSoto Hotel, 101
Dick Tracy Museum, 93–94
Dixon, 22
Dubuffet, Jean, 38
Ducks, 22
Dude ranches, 188
DuSable, Jean Baptiste Pointe, 103–4
DuSable Museum of African American
    History, 104
Dyersville, Iowa, 41–44

Eagle Creek State Park, 113–14
Eagle-watching, 162, 192, 211–13
Earp, Wyatt, 19–20

243

East Peoria, 150, 209–10
East St. Louis, 150
East Troy, Wis., 221
Eddyville, 176
Eldred, 167–68
Elephant graveyard, 23
Ellis Grove, 163, 173, 227–28
Elsah, 161, 164, 191–93
Empress I and II riverboat casinos, 151
Evanston, 9

Fall colors, 141–45
Farms, 164–66
Ferne Clyffe State Park, 144
Festival of Lights/Parade of Lights,
    209–10
Field Museum of Natural History,
    231–32
Field of Dreams cornfield stadium, 41–44
Findlay, 113–14, 114, 207–8
Finn Inn, 193
Fishing, 67
"Flamingo" (art piece), 38
Fort de Chartes State Historic Site,
    172–73
Fort Kaskaskia State Historic Site, 163,
    164, 173, 228
Four Lakes Ski Area, 221
"Four Seasons, The," 36–37
Fox Valley Canoe Trail, 129–30
Frank Lloyd Wright Home and Studio,
    237–39
Frederic C. Robie House, 239–40
"Freeform" (art piece), 38–39
French Embassy Bowling Restaurant,
    21–22
Frese, Ralph, 128

Galena, 24, 51–52, 97–102, 160, 219–20
Gambling, 70, 147–52
Garden of the Gods, 176
Gardens, 27–30
Garfield Farm, 121–25
Gays, 21
Gebhard Woods, 179
Geneseo, 24
Geneseo Historical Museum, 24
Geneva, 52, 68
Giant City State Park, 110–11, 114, 174
Gilman, 233–35
Gladioulus Festival, 30
Glencoe, 28–29
Golconda, 105, 174
Gold Coast Guest House, 52
Goose Lake Prairie State Natural Area,
    29–30, 79–82, 179–80
Gould, Chester, 94
Grafton, 113, 115, 162, 193
Grand Victoria Casino, 148–49

Great Lakes Naval Training Center, 9
Greektown, 225
Green Tree Inn, 161, 164, 192–93
Greenstone Church, 13
Grimsby, 173
Grosse Point harbor, 9
Gurnee, 61–64, 164–65

Harrisburg, 143
Harvest Feast, 183–85
Hawk watching, 206
Heartland Spa, 233–35
Hellman Guest House, 51–52, 101, 164
Hemingway, Ernest, 15–18
Hennepin Canal, 131
Herb farms, 23
Herrington Inn, 52
Historic House Museum, 19–20
Hobson, Libby and Bill, 167
Hobson's Bluffdale, 167–68
Hoopeston, 118–19
Hotel Florence, 14
Hunt, Richard, 38–39

Illinois & Michigan Canal, 177–81
Illinois Beach State Park in Zion, 9,
    66–67, 112–13, 114
Illinois St. Andrew Scottish Highland
    Games, 85–87
Illinois-Michigan Canal, 128–29
Indian Kitchen, 176
Indiana Dunes State Park and National
    Lakeshore, 71
Ingleside, 205–6
International Museum of Surgical Science
    and Hall of Fame, 201–2
Isle la Cache Museum, 179

Jaekels' Bakerie & Cafe, 100
Jean Baptiste Pointe DuSable Home and
    Trading Post Site, 103–4
John G. Shedd Aquariums, 229–30
John Hancock Center, 10
Joliet, 151
Jones, Bob and Terri, 164–65
Jug Town, 81–82
Juneteenth Day, 106

Kankakee River, 131–32
Karnak, 142
Kaskaskia Bell, 173
Kewanee, 24
Kickapoo State Park, 130–31
Kinsey Crossing Farm, 105
Kishwaukee River, 129

LaFox, 121–25
Lake Geneva, Wis., 221
Lake Michigan Circle Tour, 7–14

Lake Shelbyville Festival of Lights, 207–8
"Large Interior Form," 39
LaSalle, 180
Lawler, Robert, 47
Ledent, Jean-Louis, 22
Lemont, 178–79
Lilac Time, 30
Lincoln, Abraham, 31–34, 183–85
Lincoln Douglas Valentine Museum, 25
Lincoln Home National Historic Site, 31–32, 33
Lincoln Trail, 34
Lincoln-Herndon Law Offices State Historic Site, 32
Lindheimer Astronomical Research Center, 9
Lisle, 29, 221
Little Black Slough, 141–42
Lizzadro Museum of Lapidary Art, 203
Lockport, 179
Lombard, 30
Lusk Creek Canyon, 176

M and M Exotic Animal Walk-Through Park, 23
Mackinaw River, 132
Macomb, 23
Makanda, 110–11, 114, 174
Mansion of Golconda, 174–75
Maple Leaf Cottage Inn, 161, 164, 192
Mari-Mann Herb Farm, 23
Mary and Leigh Block Gallery, 9
Mason, Samuel, 175
McDonald's Museum, 203–4
Mendota, 117
Metra rail service, 65–72
Metropolis, 23, 77–78, 149
Michigan Avenue, North, 10–12
Michigan City, Ind., 71–72
Miller Grove Cemetery, 105
Mineral springs, 22–23
Miró, Joan, 38
Mississippi Palisades State Park, 109–10, 114
Momence, 30
Monastery Museum, 25
Monks Mound, 172
Monmouth, 19–20
Monticello, 27–28
"Monument with Standing Beast," 38
Moore, Henry, 39
Morman Church, 160–61
Morris, 29–30, 79–82, 179
Morton Arboretum, 29
Mound builders, 89–91
Mt. Morris, 112, 115
Mt. Pulaski Courthouse, 34
Mozart Festival, 93–95

Murray, Bill, 93
Museum of Collector's Plates, 203

Naper Settlement, 69–70
Naperville, 69–70
Nauvoo, 160–61, 164
New Salem State Historic Site, 34, 183–85
Nike Town, 10
North Branch of Chicago River, 132
North Chicago, 9
North Michigan Avenue, 10–12
North Point Marina, 9
North Shore, 8–9
Northern Star riverboat casino, 151
Northwestern University, 9

Oak Brook, 85–87
Oak Park, 15–18, 237–39
Oak Ridge Cemetery, 32–34
Okawville, 22
Old Courthouse Arts Center, 94
Old State Capitol, 32, 33, 104–5
Oldenburg, Claes, 36
Oliver P. Parks Telephone Museum, 25
Oquawka, 23
Oregon, 52, 187–89
Oriental Institute, 202–3
Original Mineral Springs Hotel and Bath House, 22–23
Ottawa, 180
Outhouses, 21
Owen Lovejoy Homestead, 104

Par-a-Dice, 150
Parmount Arts Centre, 70
Passion plays, 45–46
Peithman Museum, 173
Peoria, 3–6, 142–43
Pere Marquette State Park, 113, 115, 162, 164
Peru, 180
Petersburg, 34
Picasso, The, 35–36
Pick-Staiger Concert Hall, 9
Pierre Menard Home State Historic Site, 163, 164, 173
Pine Hollow Inn, 101, 164
Pinehill Bed and Breakfast Inn, 52, 188
Planetariums, 230–31
Platteville, Wis., 83–84
Players Riverboat Casino, 149–50
Postville Courthouse, 34
Pounds Hollow Lake, 175
Praire du Rocher, 172
Prairies, 79–82
Princeton, 104
Pullman, George, 12–13

Pullman Historic District, 12–14
Pumpkin festivals, 169–70

Queen Anne Guest House, 101
Quincy, 25

Railroads, 65–72
"Reading Cones," 37
Reagan, Ronald, 22
Red Cedar Trail, 174
Reed's Canoe Trips, 133
Riddle, David, 147
Robert Allerton Park, 27–28
Robie House, 239–40
Rock Island, 24, 211–13, 220
Rock Island Arsenal, 24
Rock River, 130
Rockford, 215–17
Romeoville, 179
Ronald Reagan Boyhood Home, 22
Rutherford, William, 4

St. Charles, 68–69
Sandwich, 47–48
Sandwich Antiques Market, 47–48
Scottish Highland Games, 85–87
Sears Tower, 11
Seed Savers Exchange, 121–25
Seneca Grain Elevator, 180
Serra, Richard, 37
Shawnee National Forest, 143, 173,
    175–76
Six Flags Great America, 61–64
Skiing, 219–21
Skokie Lagoon, 132
Smith, Joseph, 160–61
Snowstar Ski Area, 220
Sony's Gallery of Consumer
    Electronics, 10
Southern Star riverboat casino, 151
Spring-Shire Inn, 95
Springfield, 25, 31–34, 73–76, 240
Starved Rock State Park, 110, 115, 180
State fairs, 73–76
State parks, 109–15, 141–45
Stella, Frank, 37
Superman, 77–78
Supernatural Tours, 224
Surgical Science and Hall of Fame,
    International Museum of, 201–2
Sweet Basil Hill Farm, 164–65
Sweet corn festivals, 117–19
Sycamore, 169–70

Taetz, Patty, 192
Tamaroa, 105
Telephone museum, 25
Terra Museum of American Art, 11
Teutopolis, 25
Thanksgiving Day, 183–85
Time Museum, 215–17
"Town Ho's Story, The," 37
Tracy, Dick, 93–94
Trains, 65–72
Tribune Tower, 11
Twelfth Day of Christmas,
    227–28

Unity Temple, 239
Urbana, 117–18
Utica, 110, 115, 180

Valentines, 25
Vermillion Middle Fork, 130–31
Vernon Hills, 55–57
Villa Olivia Ski Area, 220
Vinegar Hill Historic Lead Mine and
    Museum, 24, 100–101
Volo Bog, 205–6

Warren, 23
Warren Cheese Plant, 23
Water Tower Place, 10
Wauconda, 137–39
Wauconda Orchards, 137–39
Waukegan, 67
Welles, Orson, 93
Wheaton, 53
Wheaton Inn, 53
Whistling Wings, 22
White Pines Forest State Park, 115
White Pines Ranch, 188
White Pines State Park, 112
Wildlife Prairie Park, 3–6, 142–43
Wilmette, 9–10
Wilmot, Wis., 221
Wilmot Mountain, 221
Winthrop Harbor, 9
Woodhenge, 172
Woodland Palace, 24
Woodstock, 93–95
Woodstock Mozart Festival, 93–95
Wright, Frank Lloyd, 237–41
Wrigley Building, 11
Wynne, Angus G., Jr., 61

Zion, 9, 66–67, 112–13